Don't Play Small

···

Create the Career
You Want, Deserve, and Love

···

Don't Play Small

Create the Career
You Want, Deserve, and Love

Jennifer Suarez

Published by Chiaro LLC
Reno, Nevada

Cover and interior book design by Mi Ae Lipe (whatnowdesign.com).
Back cover photo by Jordan Matter (jordanmatter.com).
Printed in the United States of America.

To contact the author or order additional copies:
Jennifer Suarez
hello@DontPlaySmall.com
DontPlaySmall.com

First Edition, July 2022
Print book ISBN: 979-8-9853009-0-1
Ebook ISBN: 979-8-9853009-1-8
Library of Congress Control Number: 2021923362

This book is dedicated to my Mom + Dad,
Judy and James Gearheart,
whose love and encouragement gave me the freedom
to walk a path that was all mine.

CONTENTS

There is no passion to be found playing small—in settling for a life that is less than the one you are capable of living.

— Nelson Mandela —

Introduction

❦

Don't play small.

It's a theme I've shared in many of my speeches over the years, and it's something that I feel strongly about. Perhaps your first reaction is that I'm asking you to find the cure to cancer, resolve the nation's debt problems, end hunger, or solve some other global issue. If one of these is your path—that's wonderful. We need you. However, that's not what I mean.

What I *am* calling on you to do, what the world needs you to do, and what you came here to do is to fully express yourself. Be who you are without reservation as you make your own unique contribution to the world. Perhaps you *are* the person who does find a cure for cancer. But perhaps your contribution is that you are an amazing parent. You could be a tremendous listener to friends who need you. You might be the best partner an individual could have in a relationship. These contributions are all parts of what you'll leave behind and be remembered for—in other words, they're part of your legacy.

This book is for those who are struggling to know and be themselves fully. As we grow into adults, we receive a lot of well-meaning guidance from parents, teachers, friends, and other influencers in our lives. But for some of you, their "good" advice has had the opposite effect and maybe even caused you to diminish yourself. Or you may be finding yourself in a situation that pushes you to be less than who you are. Or you wake up one day and find that you don't remember who you really were to begin with.

Today, most of us are in a better position to direct our lives than ever before. We're living longer. There are more and different options for where, when, and how to work. And we have the opportunity to know and understand ourselves better than before.

This book looks at how to reclaim and fully express yourself with an emphasis on your career. I focus on career because it is an important avenue that you can use to express who you are. It's where you go to show the world your talents and to have experiences that deepen and recognize your gifts.

Despite this potential, most people are not satisfied with their work. This book is aimed to help those who are not. Perhaps you don't feel passionate about or energized by the work that you do. You're not sure how to create a career or what to use for guidance. You don't know what should be considered "success" or how to measure what you're doing. Perhaps you're mired in environments in which you don't feel supported. Your life feels flat. Or perhaps you ask yourself: "Is this all there is?"

My answer is, *No, this isn't all there is—there is so much more*. I can show you—or more accurately, I can redirect you—so that you can find it within yourself. To do so, I'm going to ground you in some universal truths that will help you highlight what is important and empower you to navigate your career *your* way.

I wrote this book because I have learned how to do this for myself. I know what makes a difference. I know what separates the "success on paper" from the deep-rooted satisfaction of true success that is uniquely yours. And I know that what I'm sharing in this book are the keys to take you there.

I know because I've traveled that hard-won journey of my own, one in which I spent most of my life trying to understand how to choose and build a career. When I graduated from college in 1988, I had no idea what I wanted to do. All I knew was that I loved learning, wanted to be successful, and yearned to make a lot of money. Interestingly, this is pretty much exactly what I hear from many young professionals today.

Unfortunately, there is little to no guidance on how to do this thing we call "work." Sure, there are books about how to climb the ladder (or lattice), how to manage, or how to ask for a raise. These are valuable books. But none of them answer that one crucial question: How do I build a career that will make me happy? And when we look more deeply into our desires to be successful or wealthy, at the root of everything we discover that happiness is really what we want.

Not knowing the answer to that question (because I didn't know then that this was *the* question), I went to law school, where I excelled. I adored it. However, once I started working in the field, I did not like the practice of law. By my third year, I was crying every Sunday because I had to go to work on Monday. I didn't know what I wanted to do—I only knew what I didn't want to do.

The one thing that I did have going for me was my willingness to trust my instincts and feelings. Frankly, at the time, I felt that I was winging it in the worst sort of way. But it was the only plan I had. Little did I know that I was right to trust my instincts and that they would turn out to be one of the keys to building a happy life.

I've come a long way since then, with many achievements under my belt. I worked for a global consulting firm with over 30,000 employees, where I helped build and implement their North American sales strategy. After that, I was hired by a Fortune 100 corporation for a role created specifically for me by the CEO and the chief human resources officer. I built programs that had never existed before and built and oversaw global recruiting, learning, development, and succession planning.

I also designed and oversaw the company's first diversity program, for which I built high standards for solid goals and achievements. Part of this involved innovating new ways to identify diverse professionals for recruiting and succession planning. For example, I ensured that every key role in the company's succession plan included diverse talent on its short list, whether it came from inside our company, a different business unit, or from another company. I also reached out to competitor organizations and created agreements to share diverse recruiting candidates—if my company didn't have a spot for them, maybe theirs would and vice versa. I was also the first person to tie diversity achievements to the bonuses of this company's leaders.

Over the past twenty-seven years, I've interviewed and helped hire and promote people for thousands of jobs. Along the way, I've worked with and coached more senior executives than I can count. The same goes for college grads and entry-level and mid-career professionals as well.

Because I so keenly remember my own early struggles, I've always come into these relationships truly caring about the individual and trying to understand what makes them different and what kind of a role in which they'd thrive. This openness and caring has, I believe, allowed me extraordinary insight into the decisions people make—what drives their choices, what has worked, what hasn't, and how it all fits together.

In short, I've learned a tremendous amount about how to craft a career that incorporates all of you. A career that can make you happy. A career in which you thrive. A career that allows you to access the loyal, always available, truthful, and devoted guide that lies within you.

This is your life. Let me show you how you can be the CEO of it, no matter what age you are. If you're like me—fifty or older—let me show you how to recognize the signposts that point you to the ways you can choose to deliver your legacy.

But, to do these things, you need to stand in your power.

You need to reclaim and celebrate all the parts that are uniquely you. Don't play small. You are much greater than you have ever imagined. And the time to claim this greatness for yourself is now.

There is no greater agony
than bearing an untold story inside you.

— Maya Angelou —

LIFE TRUTHS

THIS IS A BOOK ABOUT YOUR CAREER. The word "career" packs *so* many unrecognized expectations because your career is an expression of yourself. Hopefully, it is a place where your gifts can come out and shine. It is often one of the yardsticks to measure how you're doing in the world. It is also probably where you hope to secure resources for yourself and the other lives you support. (No wonder then if you're stressed out about your career!)

This book can help you sort through these expectations and prioritize them. It's a lot simpler than you think, and it takes much less contemplation than you might imagine. In fact, I'm going to ask the "thinking" part of you to get quiet for a moment, suspend judgment, and be open to a few ideas.

First, you're going learn a lot of information that you may not have learned in traditional get-ahead-in-business books. In fact, the advice in this book may feel completely counterintuitive and out-of-the-box. That's good. You shouldn't be in a box anyway. I have the experience, and I *know* that what I'm preaching here works. What I'm giving you in this book are not theories, but two Life Truths validated by thousands upon thousands of examples I've witnessed as well as experienced firsthand. I also share examples; although the names and identifying information in them have been changed to protect every person's confidentiality, they are all based on actual people and experiences.

Second, some of what I tell you may sound "woo-woo." I get that. I'm a left-brained lawyer. I rely on facts and supporting evidence. But the facts and evidence behind what I say are events I've witnessed again and again. Moreover, I imagine that most of you will feel the truth of my insights when you hear them.

If you're on the fence with a few of the ideas, I urge you to suspend your judgment. Give them a shot. What have you got to lose? They're all focused on your success. They're all focused on your happiness. They are based on the experiences of someone who has focused on human talent and professional development for almost her entire career. They are from someone who's been there and done it—and who's helped others do it as well. If you are willing to give these ideas a try, your only risk is that you become a *little* happier and more successful. Then again, you could find that your life becomes newly defined by the happiness and success that you have created. Either one is a pretty good payoff.

I've seen these Life Truths at work in careers at all levels and stages across the board. Each Life Truth is a distillation of a trait that has made someone wildly successful, the thing that someone needed to work on in order to achieve success. I call them Life Truths because, even though we're talking about business, they apply to all aspects of life. Since this book is primarily about your career, we'll stick to business for now.

The two Life Truths each contain five key principles. Here's a table you can refer to for a quick reminder any time.

LIFE TRUTH 1: SUCCESS IS AN INSIDE JOB

- Your Goals Must Align with Your Inner Values
- You Portray to the World What Is Inside of You
- The Primary Beneficiary of Your Integrity Is You
- Love and Kindness Are Stronger than Anything Else
- Your Intuition Speaks to You through Your Body

LIFE TRUTH 2: YOU ARE HERE TO LEAVE A LEGACY

- A Career Is an Evolution
- It's Never about the Money
- Mistakes Are Full of Opportunities
- Leaving Is Just as Important as a Promotion
- Don't Let Others Shrink You

DON'T PLAY SMALL.

Be all of you,
with kindness and compassion,
all of the time.

LIFE TRUTH 1:
SUCCESS IS AN INSIDE JOB

Your time is limited,
so don't waste it living someone else's life.

Don't be trapped by dogma,
which is living the results of other people's thinking.

Don't let the noise of others' opinions
drown out your own inner voice.

And most important, have the courage
to follow your heart and intuition.

They somehow already know
what you truly want to become.

— Steve Jobs —

THIS MAY BE THE MOST IMPORTANT TRUTH you need to know. Why? Because understanding this truth and its related principles will empower you unlike anything else. Gone is the insecurity of not knowing what to choose for yourself. These principles help you build a strong inner life where you know yourself, you can trust your inner guidance on decisions, and you have built a way of being in the world that contributes to your inner strength.

What do I mean by inner life, inner guidance, and inner strength? Let's take them one by one.

Inner life refers to things such as your hopes, dreams, thoughts, and emotions. These are all intangibles that exist inside of you. Having a strong and rich inner life means that you can identify and understand their unique importance for yourself. For example, I may have the dream of living in New York City and raising a family there, or your dreams may be to live in your hometown or travel the world.

Your thoughts and emotions are unique to you as well. What makes you happy or angry may not be the same as for someone else. Moreover, as I explain in the section on intuition, understanding your emotions is key to accessing your intuition. In many ways, once you understand these qualities about your inner life and the principles in this section, they become the foundational sources that inform your inner guidance.

So, what is *inner guidance*? When you're faced with a choice, such as whether you should take a particular job, you will naturally look for ways on how to make that best decision. You may consult with your family or colleagues; when you do, this is asking for outer guidance, meaning external guidance from others. You may also look within yourself to evaluate what you want. Does this job fit into a long-term dream you are working toward? How do you feel about the work, the people, and the company? What are your thoughts as you analyze the attributes of the position and weigh how it fits you?

....

Until you learn to name your ghosts
and to baptize your hopes,
you have not yet been born;
you are still the creation of others.

— Maria Cardinal, *The Words to Say It* —

....

This dialogue with yourself is you tapping into sources that inform your inner guidance. When we really understand ourselves, our inner guidance becomes a deeply trusted source that helps us make decisions that we know are in our best interests and align with us perfectly. Developing a rich inner life creates the confidence to follow your internal knowing and guidance. It becomes your personal compass.

Now, let's add *inner strength*. Inner strength describes your confidence in relying on your inner guidance system for answers. The more of this you have, the more solid you are in your decisions. You simply *know* the right choice to make. You are confident, regardless of whether or not your decision is contrary to what others think.

Inner strength is also something that you build. The more you know yourself and trust making decisions using your inner guidance, the stronger your inner strength becomes. And, as I explain later, inner strength grows as you make choices to live in integrity because honesty and truth create strength. It also flourishes when you choose to act in love and kindness as you live your life.

These three concepts interlink and build upon one another. As you come to know yourself more, you make better decisions by trusting your guidance. As you trust your inner guidance more and have the positive experiences of how it supports you, you build your inner strength. All three have to do with what is inside of you. And they create the foundation for your success.

The five principles for this inner truth inform you on how to use this foundation. For example, success—meaning success that resonates with you, that is lasting and that fuels your happiness—has to be defined from inside of you, not by some outside measure that someone else holds up to you. This ability to define it from inside yourself requires that you know yourself and your values—that is, your inner life. Aligning your achievements with markers that match your values lets you accomplish the feeling of success in a lasting way. In contrast, the external markers of success—that is, those based on what others deem "successful"—fail to give you this lasting experience.

Your emotions, which also stem from your inner life, are a very important part of who you are. Mistakenly, many people have been taught that having emotions and feelings is a weakness in business. In fact, it's the opposite. Understanding one's emotions is what makes the difference between an average leader and a great one, and between someone who looks good on paper to someone who feels deeply successful and confident. Emotions are a source of information and intelligence that informs your guidance system. It's imperative to know this part of yourself because, without it, you don't have access to your intuition. When you ignore emotions, it doesn't mean they aren't active, because they are. They emanate from you and inform others because you project your feelings and thoughts, consciously and unconsciously.

In other words, if you're nervous, angry, or confused, you are sending that message whether or not you actually say anything—in every moment of the day, in every interview, meeting, or luncheon. This form of nonverbal communication is unavoidable. That's why you need to know and pay attention to what is going on inside of you as you build a strong inner life.

With this backdrop, let's explore each of the five principles.

YOUR GOALS MUST ALIGN
WITH YOUR INNER VALUES

*Success is only meaningful and enjoyable
if it feels like your own.*

— Michelle Obama —

EXTERNAL MARKERS OF SUCCESS (meaning achievements that others say define success) ring hollow if they do not align with your internal markers (achievements that align with what's really important to you). In other words, a goal has to mean something to your personal value system.

This is the harder, possibly more elusive part of goal setting. Why? Internal markers require that we actually know what has meaning and value to us. But what if you have not been taught how to build an inner relationship with yourself? An inner relationship is one where you learn and listen to what really matters to you. Without this ability, you are left with intellectualizing about what you "should" strive for as a goal. You may end up choosing what society and others deem a success. The problem is that such goals can feel flat—they become just another item on a checklist. At best, achieving them can give you only a momentary sense of accomplishment.

In contrast, when you have a goal that matches your internal values, you *feel* that achievement. It's not just a fleeting idea or moment. Moreover, you reexperience the feeling every time you reflect back on that particular success. That's how you know that the goal truly matched your internal values. It's also how you will have successes that truly matter.

So, what are values? You may have heard of "corporate values," which are considered foundational blocks on which a company builds its policies and products and uses to govern its philosophy, strategy and decision-making. For example, corporate values could include equality, trust, and innovation. For individuals, values can be defined as something that you believe is important in life or a standard of living to which you hold yourself. For example, my values include integrity, self-trust, and loyalty, among others. Here's an example of how a goal matched one of my values.

External markers of success are achievements that others say define success; internal markers align with what's really important to you.

When I lived in Ohio, I started running simply for fitness and as a way to relieve stress. At one point, when I was up to eight miles a day, I saw a sign for the Columbus Marathon. I had never heard of a marathon and didn't know what it was. When my best friend told me that it was a run of more than twenty-six miles, I decided that I was in!

I loved running and wanted to see if I could complete a marathon. My friend gently tried to talk sense into me—people trained months for these and the Columbus one was just two weeks away. Yet, those words made me want to do it even more.

Why did I want to do it? To test my stamina—sure. But mostly, I refused to be told I couldn't do something. I wanted to do it because I felt exhausted by the rules and limitations expressed by others. I wanted to see if I was capable of doing it just because I *wanted* to do it, to simply push through whatever it required and, as a result, know that I could do anything I set my heart on. The underlying value at stake was believing in myself.

It took me over four hours, but I finished the marathon. A profound sense of accomplishment and success permeated my entire body. I was floating. I'm still floating just thinking about it! It's an example of where the marker of running a marathon perfectly matched an internal value I had.

Years later in New York City, I was still running marathons. The first time I ran the NYC Marathon, there was still that sense of accomplishment. It felt good. However, I didn't feel this way after completing it the last two times. In fact, I felt incredibly flat emotionally. Yes, I liked that I could talk about it, and I liked that I could say that I "did it." But this time, the sense of accomplishment was not the same at the end, and even that feeling didn't last. That's when I knew that completing a marathon no longer matched an inner sense of value for me—it had turned into an item on a checklist. And I realized it was time to stop.

You probably grew up thinking a lot about what you wanted to "be." Perhaps, in thinking about the future "successful" version of yourself, you thought of titles and achievements—external markers that you were taught would be valuable if you achieved something. You heard about them from your parents, other family members, teachers, peers, friends, and the media. These markers have been deeply ingrained and hardwired into your thinking. So, you naturally chose them as measures of what you should attain.

But there are two inherent problems with using external markers to measure your success.

External Markers Fail Because the Experience or Feeling of Success Comes from the Inside

The experience of success is a feeling state. Calling it a "feeling state," of course, begs the question of *how do I get there* and *how do I feel what I want to feel?* Great! I'm glad you asked.

It's an inside job.

The first requirement is that you be willing to reflect, look inside, and listen to what *does* have meaning to you. You have to form your *own* definition of success. This definition is *always* based on values and feelings—no matter what the goals are. You may set a goal of becoming a manager because you *think* this will make you feel successful. While this goal-setting method can sometimes be effective, it is backward and narrow, especially in the long term. A more expansive array of possible goals opens up once you can describe the *essence* of what you want (that is, the feeling state you want to experience) and you're able look at all the possible ways to achieve those feelings.

So, start with the feelings, not the goals. For example, you might want to feel effective in developing and growing people in a team by becoming a manager. With this in mind, you can consider a much broader range of experiences to achieve this goal, not just a single experience linked to a managerial title. You can also broaden the way you become and operate as a manager. Achieving the goal of such a title can be a checklist item; however, achieving the goal of effectively developing and growing other people, whether as a manager or not, can be life-changing for everyone involved.

You also need to include in your personal definition of success all the meaningful areas of your life and what success will look like in each area. Many of you may have been trained to compartmentalize your lives: work, family, parenthood, friends, etc. You may have an idea of what you want from your work. You may have even made a list of things to do for your family. Yet, you may not have looked at the big picture of how each area—for you personally—is prioritized against the other and what success means within each of them. Focusing on isolated, distinct areas of your life without understanding or linking them in the big picture is a narrow approach to life that inevitably stops working.

Let me give you an example. Amy runs a division of a company. She's an innovator and change leader who has led her division to record profits. As a result, she's been asked to be on corporate boards and nonprofit committees, and she's received many other worldly accolades. When she was just turning fifty, she told me that, despite this fabulous career—for which she is very proud and grateful—something is missing. She couldn't put her finger on it yet, but she didn't feel successful, even though the rest of the world views her that way.

When we talked through the areas of her life, she began to build some insight. She has wonderful friends. She has been the mother she wanted to be. She's traveled as much as she's ever dreamed of doing. However, we discovered that she felt empty in two major areas of her life. The first is that she longs to be in a true partnership. She is divorced and hasn't had the time or focus to develop a relationship. The second is that she feels a deep commitment to her religious background. She is Jewish and passionately believes in giving back to her heritage. In fact, as we delved deeper, it became apparent that her heritage is one of her highest values. She has built a life that does not include this part of her in a way that she deems successful. Is it any wonder that she doesn't fully feel her success? She's left out a major piece of what she desires to experience in order to personally feel successful.

The point is that it's never too late to take an inventory of your values and the things that hold meaning in your life. I advocate that we all do it periodically over the course of our lives, because what we value can change or our priorities can change. For instance, if you're a single person just starting out in your career, family may not even be on your list yet. You may feel that your career is the area that holds the biggest value and you want to focus on building it because, after you succeed, you will *feel* like a provider. Then, from this place of feeling that you can provide, you might be ready to add the family component. The point is to know thyself so you can build a strong inner life. And this means checking in with yourself from time to time to know how you're evolving and whether anything has changed.

External Markers Fail in Striving Cultures

We live in a "striving" culture. This means that we're goal-oriented and future-directed. We strive to get this and accomplish that, always extending our mental and chronological calendars. In fact, most of us have a very hard time being in the present moment. What happens with this mindset is that you set a goal—an external marker that you want to meet—and once you meet it, you immediately set a new goal. Or worse, when you're close to meeting the goal, you change the finish line. That means you're always chasing the future but not enjoying, or even acknowledging, what you've achieved once you got there.

Here are a couple examples of how this can happen.

Joe was an entry-level hire in the sales department. He was bright and highly motivated and doing a great job. However, his passion was writing; in fact, he was completing a master's degree in this field. After two years of doing sales, Joe secured a role in his company's communications department, a position that was rarely available. Joe was ecstatic . . . for about four months. Instead of allowing himself to fully *feel* the satisfaction of attaining a role where he was paid to write, settling into his job, and maximizing its experience for the next few years, all he could think about was his next move or promotion and how to plan for it.

Here's another example: Carla was hired to run a new Internet business. In her first year, she built a core team, launched new products, and generated millions of dollars in revenue. It was deemed a highly successful year. For her second year, her boss set a revenue target of almost ten million dollars, which everyone agreed would be a real stretch to achieve. Yet, by midway through the year, Carla and her team were on target to hit this ambitious goal. Terrific—right? But her boss and the senior executive team thought they must have set the bar too low. So, they upped the revenue target for the year—in other words, they moved the finish line.

Moving the target goal was unfair. It might have caused Carla and her team to lose their motivation; after all, why keep trying if the goal is always moving away? But changing the goal near the finish line happens all the time. And it's not just something that happens *to* us. We're often the ones doing the goal changing to ourselves. We've been trained this way in life and in our jobs. We get close to losing ten pounds and then we decide that fifteen pounds would be better. We believe we'll feel like we've "made" it when we get that two-bedroom home and new car. Yet, once we have it, we tell ourselves that what we really meant was a four-bedroom home on two acres and a *luxury* car. The bait-and-switch that we allow to happen at the office reflects what we as a society have accepted as a norm. But the truth is, if we didn't accept it so readily, it wouldn't happen.

The result: In a striving culture, we rarely get (or allow ourselves) to experience the success of the external marker we chose. We either set ourselves up so that we never reach the goal, or we don't stop to acknowledge that we did meet it. In contrast, when you set a goal that aligns with your internal values, it's not just an item on a list that lacks an anchor, but it's rooted in something meaningful to you. Therefore, you're not likely to simply change it. You'll go for it with heart and, trust me, you will feel and own it when you reach it.

YOU PORTRAY TO THE WORLD
WHAT IS INSIDE OF YOU

❦

Realize that now, in this moment of time,
you are creating.

You are creating your next moment based on
what you are feeling and thinking.

That is what's real.

— Doc Childre, founder of HeartMath Institute —

I HAVE SEEN THIS PRINCIPLE at work so much that to me, it is as obvious and real as the grass is green and the sky is blue. Everything you are feeling and thinking in any given moment is being projected out into and portrayed to the world. In its own way, what is inside is actually manifested on the outside.

The underlying reason for why you are projecting yourself this way is that we are energetic beings. Our thoughts create emotions, and our emotions project outward from us. Candace Pert, the former section chief of brain biochemistry at the National Institute of Mental Health, researched this and found that our emotions not only change our own body chemistry, but **they also change the body chemistry of the people we interact with**.

Our emotions send electrical signals that travel not just to the receptors on our own body cells but also on the cells of other people nearby. Pert said, "We're not just little hunks of meat. We're vibrating like a tuning fork—we send out a vibration to other people. We broadcast and receive. [We] are connected to everybody else."[1]

In the movie *I Am,* a documentary by Tom Shadyac, the award-winning director of movies such as *Liar Liar* and *Ace Ventura: Pet Detective,* there's a scene where Tom works with the HeartMath Institute to test whether emotions can impact another living being. Tom is seated at a table; across from him is a glass petri dish filled with plain yogurt. The yogurt contains live cultures and is connected via electrodes to an analog voltmeter, which measures energy (or reactions to energy) from the yogurt. All of the electronics in the room, such as watches and phones, have been turned off, and all forms of electromagnetic interference are controlled so as not to impact the experiment. As Tom is asked to think about highly emotional events (such as his divorce), the voltmeter shoots up—the energy in the yogurt spikes exactly when his emotions do. This experiment suggests that our emotions do emit energies and affect those around us.

No doubt, you may find this experiment far-fetched; it certainly had critics. But when you think about it, you can find instances where you've personally experienced the emotional energy that another person was emitting. Maybe it was a time when you walked into the room and someone important to you was really mad at you, and the air was thick with the intensity of their emotions. We can and do feel the emotions that others project. And they can feel our emotions too—whether they're good or bad.

People are picking up on emotions and reacting to them all the time. In fact, they pick up on your energetic messaging and translate it into an understanding before you even open your mouth and before their brains kick in enough to intellectualize what's going on.

These concepts are confirmed by Tor Nørretranders, author of *The User Illusion: Cutting Consciousness Down to Size,* in which he provides a scientifically based explanation of how people experience more than they are consciously aware of. He shares that, by the 1980s, it became clear that "most of the information that passes through a person is not picked up by their consciousness," including information we act upon.[2] He further states that "we actually know more about what other people think and feel than our consciousness does. So, what we think and feel about each other does matter…"[3]

THE SINGLE MOST IMPORTANT PART OF AN INTERVIEW

I've often been asked to speak on how to interview well. I have interviewed thousands of people for all kinds of positions, from junior level to division heads and even chief financial officers. Yes, I review their résumés first to see if they have credentials for the job. And I've often had an initial phone call with them or had them screened by someone else. But I always insist on a face-to-face interview because it allows me to assess the one thing that tells me what I really need to know.

It is how they walk into the room.

For proper context, you need to know the type of interviewer that I am. I am not the kind who expects you to prove yourself to me. Nor do I think that interviewing is an inconvenience for me and I want to get it over with as soon as possible. Either approach would influence the way that you, as the candidate, react to me. I'm aware of this and avoid giving such impressions.

I *love* meeting people and understanding what they are all about. I make sure that I'm providing a positive atmosphere where you can feel comfortable talking to me. So, when candidates walk into my office, they are stepping into a warm environment, where they can feel that they have the freedom to be their best (or worst).

What are the two biggest mistakes that people make when they interview for a job? The first mistake is when the person is overly eager for the job yet insecure about getting it (or insecure about themselves). I see this frequently. You may be interviewing for a role you're deeply interested in and nervous because you want it so much. You want the interviewer to "get you" and value what you've done. Perhaps you've never met the interviewer before, and you want them to like you. You want them to confirm that you're qualified and perfect—but you don't completely believe it yourself. Instead of acknowledging to yourself that you are nervous and insecure, you push those feelings aside and go in trying to "sell" yourself.

The problem is, your unacknowledged insecurity can come across as desperate and not in sync with what you're verbally communicating. This makes the other person nervous. They become confused by your energy because they're subconsciously picking up on your insecurities and are internalizing your messages of "I'm not sure I'm qualified, I'm afraid you won't think so." And thus, your energy undermines your strengths. I could be the most talented woman in the world, but if I'm nervously pushing myself on you by telling you how desperately I want to work for you, you're probably not going to hire me because, consciously or unconsciously, most of us avoid desperate or nervous people. They're not comfortable to be around.

The second interviewing mistake is to mask insecurity by being overly cocky. By this, I don't mean someone who is simply confident and energetic. This type of strategy involves an overabundance of aggressiveness. Such people project energy, whether they truly feel this way or not, that comes across like they're too good for the role or that the interviewer is lucky to be spending time with them at all. Their underlying insecurity may lead them to name-drop, as in "oh do you know so-and-so?" ("because I do and you better take note"). This confusing mix of aggression and insecurity results in an interviewer not wanting to help them, much less work with them.

Both of these types express themselves just by how they walk into the room. I know how they will present before they even open their mouths, because their feelings and thoughts precede them energetically and are displayed in their actions.

With the eager but insecure person, I can detect that they are on edge, energetically. There is a frantic, nervous quality about them that makes me feel compelled to reassure them that they are okay. Such a person has difficulty standing straight. They enter the room quietly and try not to disturb its energy. They may have a hard time looking me in the eye. When they do, I can see their nervousness.

I have a lot of compassion for this type of candidate. I've been there—we've all been there. As I talk to them and they relax a bit, they eventually open up to how much they want the job and all the crazy thoughts they're thinking, such as their worthiness for the position (however fragile they might feel) and the nervousness that they're experiencing internally. But I knew all this already—from the moment they entered my office.

In contrast, the cocky person walks in and projects that they own all the space in my office. They survey the room as if they're judging it. Their energy feels like they think they are better than me (which is a very curious and strange experience when I'm the one deciding whether they go further)! They puff out their chest. They stare hard at me. I almost want my assistant to sit in the room to make sure I stay safe.

Invariably, this person's inner dialogue falls into one of two camps. The first one is that they are just as nervous as our eager person, but they've been taught to play overconfident. That overconfidence is not based on how that person is truly feeling inside, so it comes off as cocky. The second camp is that the person has been taught that they need pump themselves up to believing that they *are* the best and they must "own" the situation. The result is that they have worked themselves up into believing that they need to think or act that they were too good to have to even interview; thus, their inner dialogue precisely mirrors their outer projection.

I share these examples to drive home the point that you are projecting yourself *the moment you enter the room*. As soon as we meet, you're giving off energy and I'm reading it. Your energy is made up of all the thoughts that are running through your head at that moment and in the moments leading up to the encounter.

For news of the heart, ask the face.

— West African saying —

To help you prepare for interviews, I want to share some fundamental energy skills that I learned through my work with horses. In my consulting practice, I've used horses to help executives understand what they are portraying nonverbally. Horses are perfect mirrors because they don't really care what we're saying—they're reading what we're projecting via our inner dialogue of feelings and thoughts. They are also social animals who are inclined to want someone in the herd—but only if that individual is trustworthy and safe. These same principles apply to humans.

As I just said, the herd will accept someone who is trustworthy and safe. At a minimum, this requires that a person is "emotionally congruent," which means that you are aware of your feelings and accept them, and that you are acting in accordance with them. In general, horses accept someone who is nervous. You just need to acknowledge (to yourself) that you are indeed feeling nervous, accept that feeling and thought, and then move forward as solidly as you can with that knowing. Your inner dialogue might be, "I really want this job and I'm feeling nervous about this interview." Just add to it, "I'm not going to fight the fact that I'm feeling nervous. I'm going to accept it and go in and do my best." This is congruent and honest. Moreover, it gives you *strength*. The result is that you begin to portray energetically to me your integrity and strength.

Being willing to go to the edge of discomfort, notice it without having to change it, and move forward in spite of it creates an inner sense of confidence and possibility. It reprograms the way in which we previously acted out or avoided situations because of our discomfort by creating a pattern of courage that becomes a new way of behaving for you.

For instance, Jolie is a singer who always feels nervous before she performs, which feels like butterflies fluttering almost uncontrollably within her. But, instead of trying to push away that nervous feeling, make it wrong, or act like it doesn't exist, she allows it to sit in her body. In fact, after working with it for so long, she now describes it as embracing the force of energy that the emotion is creating. She realized that it is her body understanding her need to ramp up her energy so she can project it out to her audience and meet the energy that they're in turn projecting back to her. In other words, she's learned that when she embraces her nervousness, it actually fuels and empowers her singing and performance. She has discovered how to be emotionally congruent with this energy.

Getting back to horses, there are two situations in which they won't accept your nervousness. First, if you're caught up in your nervous energy and it's running you (that is, your mind is sprinting with crazy thoughts that are affecting your emotions), your out-of-control emotional state makes you come across as unsafe. You need to tame that out-of-control state by identifying and accepting your emotions and either embracing them like

Jolie or simply acknowledging they're present and acting in spite of it. Otherwise, when you ignore your emotions and allow them to churn wildly, horses (and humans) want to get away from you quickly because you're unsafe to the herd.

Second, if you are nervous but act in a manner inconsistent with that emotion (that is, you try to be overconfident and don't acknowledge your nervousness), a horse won't come near you. They'll consider you a weak and dangerous member of the herd because of your incongruency. This means you're acting and communicating one thing, but your emotions—and therefore energy—are communicating something contrary. Instinctively, it feels like you're lying and therefore untrustworthy.

Horses also won't accept aggression. *Confidence* is fine. In fact, they love true confidence because that means you might be a good leader. A good leader to a horse is someone who is confident but also calm, aware of everything around them, and willing to consider and care for the herd. So, if you're running on arrogance, you may have some congruency and confidence, but you aren't calm and acting like you care about the herd's welfare. Thus, you have turned into a predator and are fundamentally not to be trusted.

Simply put: You need to be aware of what you're feeling at all times. Accept whatever those emotions are (quietly in your mind is sufficient) and move confidently (not cockily) in the direction you want to go—be it an interview, a staff meeting, a board meeting, or simply lunch with a colleague.

THE PRIMARY BENEFICIARY
OF YOUR INTEGRITY IS YOU

Integrity is your destiny.
It is the light that guides your way.

— Plato —

ANOTHER PRINCIPLE OF LIFE TRUTH 1 relates to the importance of integrity.

No doubt you have been told that you should have integrity. That integrity is the mark of a good person. So, as with many moral certitudes, you may believe that it is something you should do because it's the right thing to do. That's true. But I'm going to give you a very selfish reason to have integrity: Integrity serves you. It strengthens you. It empowers you. Morality apart, the primary reason you should have integrity is because of how it affects—in a very positive, powerful way—yourself.

What is integrity anyway? Here's how the Merriam-Webster dictionary defines integrity:

1. *Firm adherence to a code of especially moral or artistic values: incorruptibility*

2. *An unimpaired condition: soundness*

3. *The quality or state of being complete or undivided: completeness*

Many would say that it includes honesty. I would agree that honesty certainly fits into adherence to a code of moral values. Yet it's bigger than that. Integrity is about your own honor code of what you will and won't do. While that code must contain things like honesty, it should include other values that are meaningful to you as well as the promises you make.

The Strength of Honesty

Let's start with why honesty is a must. Dr. David Hawkins, in his book *Power vs. Force: The Hidden Determinants of Human Behavior*, describes how he was able to demonstrate that our body is a truth machine from over twenty years of kinesiology research. He found that untruths, or lies, *physically weaken* the body, while the body literally grows stronger with the truth.[4]

Try it for yourself using the following common kinesthetic method. You can use it to test for the truth of a declarative statement made (meaning that you're testing to see if the statement is true or false). A declarative statement is a sentence that basically declares something, like "The sky is blue" or "I am forty-eight years old" or even "I didn't eat the last slice of pie."

The test itself is a simple arm test that you can do with your friends at home (or with colleagues at the office party and really wow them). You'll need two people: you as the tester and a second person who'll be your partner. This second person is the one who will make the declarative statement. Here's how it works:

1. Have your partner extend their dominant arm (the one that they write with) straight out in front of them. They must hold it as strongly as they can. Their goal throughout the experiment is to keep you from pushing it down.

2. Take your dominant hand and, using two fingers, try to push their arm down. You may be able to push it down only a little bit. That's okay. You're testing to see how much force you need to move it.

3. Next, test a statement that you know is true. While your partner is still holding their arm out straight and resisting your downward push, have them say something truthful in a declarative statement. For example: "My name is _____."

4. *While* they are speaking (this is key), try to push down their arm. It will be noticeably harder to push it down.

5. Next, test something that's untrue. While your partner is still holding their arm out straight and resisting you, have them say a lie, something like "I like to eat dirt" (or worms or any other gross thing that you know isn't true).

6. Try pushing their arm down while they're saying this lie. You should find it incredibly easier. They may ask you to do it again because they might think they weren't ready. They were. Their bodies were just responding to the lie or untruth.

Try it a few times just to be sure. Try it on your kids. Ask your son to say "I didn't start the fight," and push his arm down to test if it's true. (Once I started using this technique, my boys started coming clean a lot sooner on what really happened.)

Bodies are our personal lie detector tests. Your body loves the truth and is strengthened by it. Lies weaken the body, including little white lies. The more you live in honesty, the stronger you become. This is an absolute.

The Importance of Promises

This brings me to the importance of promises. Living life means that you will at some point—probably many points—make a commitment. You'll promise to take out the garbage, get a report in by Friday, stop smoking, you name it. Promises are woven into being in relationships with others and ourselves.

There is something profoundly important about promises and keeping them. You can almost tangibly feel how they build trust when you keep them or erode trust when you don't. And, in turn, kept promises contribute to your core strength.

Therefore, when you make promises, you need to be very sure about them. When you tell the boss that they will get something by ten o'clock tomorrow morning, you must make sure they get it by then. And you must make sure (for you, if nobody else) that it's exactly as you said it would be. Similarly, when you tell your employee that you're going to put them on a special project, you need to follow through and do it. And it needs to be the exact project that you discussed and in the timeframe that you named for it.

Your track record for keeping these promises (or not) are what people look at to determine if they can rely on you. It communicates if you're reliable. This gives you even more reason to make sure you're clear about—with others and yourself—exactly what you're promising.

Just because keeping promises is important doesn't mean you always have to keep the promise—come hell or high water, regardless of the impact—once you've made it. There are sometimes very good reasons why a promise can't be met or has to be met differently. The key is to come clean that the promise was made, but you can no longer (or simply won't) keep it. You can add what you're willing to recommit to doing, if anything. And you can add "why" if you want.

I know that socially or emotionally you may feel that you need to soften the way you communicate the change in a promise, for the other person or yourself. However, the "why" (whether it's justified or not) seems to be less important from a truth perspective than simply owning up to the fact that you made the promise and that you are uncommitting. Integrity means owning what the promise was and that you have changed your mind—for whatever reason. This is honesty through and through.

It is also just as important that you handle the promises you make to *yourself* this way. Maybe it's even more important, as you may be the one person with whom you break promises the most often. How many times have you promised yourself that you'd commit to exercise? Lose weight? Ask for a raise? Write that book?

We make promises all the time to ourselves and then renege on them. Or ignore them. Or procrastinate (which is basically the same thing). But we rarely go back and come clean with ourselves. We never go back, acknowledge that we said we were going to do something, uncommit from that promise, and say what, if anything, we may be willing to recommit to do.

This failure to acknowledge and revisit promises is one of our biggest undoings. Because when we make a promise to ourselves and then don't keep it, we are telling *ourselves* that we are untrustworthy. I have coached innumerable executives who want something and then lose (or lack) the confidence that they can do it. They want a new job. They want a promotion. They want to hit a new sales target. But deep down, they actually believe they can't.

One of the biggest contributors to such insecurity and lack of faith in self occurs when we no longer believe ourselves. The unconscious self has experienced us making promises to ourselves and reneging too many times to have faith that we will actually follow through. Remember, it doesn't happen over-night. It builds up. And it's a pattern that is deadly to success.

If you don't trust yourself implicitly on a subconscious level, you will act out these insecurities and miss opportunities. Promises kept are of dire importance in every conversation that you have with yourself. When you can't keep the promise that you made, come clean with yourself.

Coming clean is similar to being emotionally congruent with a herd of horses. You don't have to be herculean. You don't have to move mountains if you've made a promise under one set of circumstances and they've changed, if you've mis-judged your ability, or if you simply have changed your mind. Again, the reason that you want to uncommit is unimportant. What *is* important is that the promise is acknowledged.

Cleanup is as simple as the following: *I know I promised myself that I would stop drinking coffee this week. However, I now realize that there is too much happening this week to work through the caffeine withdrawal. (Or I realize that I love coffee and don't want to stop having it.) So, I formally uncommit from that promise and will look at it again when I'm more ready, if ever.* Period.

When you can live your life with this kind of integrity—toward other people and yourself—then you will achieve the state of integrity described by Merriam-Webster: soundness and completeness. Being sound and complete in your own right and from within—that is true strength.

Love and Kindness Are Stronger than Anything Else

✦❦✦

The sun never says to the earth, "You owe me."

Look what happens with a love like that—
it lights up the whole sky.

— Hafiz, Persian poet and mystic —

What I find fascinating about many career books is the implicit or explicit guidance to be a hard-liner person. Kick ass and take no prisoners. Tell them who's boss. Be tough. Fight your way to the top.

I vehemently disagree.

A couple of years ago, I participated in a mentoring round-table. The mentors were selected senior professionals who had been asked to mentor high-performing young professionals who were the first in their family to go to college. The mentees were tops in their graduating class. They were in positions with leading organizations and recognized by those companies as doing terrific jobs. They were also members of minority groups who might not have had some of the mentoring infrastructures available to others. As the only one from my family who went to college, I was like them; I had had to learn the ropes of how to advance my career on my own. I was excited to share what I had learned.

At the culminating dinner, there were intimate breakout panels where each executive would sit with several of these young professionals, who could ask any question on their minds.

When I sat down with my second group, there was a young, vibrant woman who anyone would say was totally "together." She was driven, self-motivated, warm, and loved by all—justifiably. She proceeded to tell me about a book she had read that was written for people starting their career and how it advised them that they had to be ruthless. She wanted my perspective on whether this is what I saw and if you really had to be "mean" to get ahead (her word).

I told her to burn that book.

I have rarely seen anyone get ahead through ruthless methods. Oh, it happens. We can all cite one case at least. But in my experience, it is the least effective path. Every success I've ever experienced was made easier through warmth, kindness, and—dare I say—love. Yes, I'll go ahead and say it. *Love*.

In my first job in Manhattan, I was a traditional headhunter at an agency where my job was to cold call companies and prospective professionals. Cold calling is where you call someone who's never met or heard of you and try to get them to speak to you. Because you're a stranger, the percentage of people who are willing to take your call is very low. Yet, right from the start, I had the highest callback rate that anyone in my office had ever heard of: ninety percent. I had two Fortune 500 clients within my first year. Unheard of!

Why was I so successful? I was nice. *Nice*. I'm not saying that because that's what I think I was. Clients and candidates told me again and again that it was *the* reason they called me back. They told me that when they listened to my voicemail messages, they could tell that I was a nice person. It was the *primary* reason they responded to me.

The same holds true for other major accomplishments that I've had. When I was a senior manager at a global consulting firm, I was responsible for a monthly report that went to the firm's board of directors. The report measured three of the firm's strategic initiatives using metrics that pulled information from all parts of the firm, including different technology systems and files from the desks of too many people to count. The data gathering alone was deemed an insurmountable task because it had never been done before.

But I and my team did it. Every month and on time. How did we do it? We were *nice*. From the beginning and with every interaction, I was nice. I collaborated. I treated people with respect. Because of this, they wanted to help me. They gave me the data I needed on time.

In that project, I met several partners who are some of the most outstanding individuals I've ever known. What made them stand out? Yes, they were brilliant and influential. But they were also caring and nice. This quality of niceness endeared them to everyone, including me. They made me want to give them *my* best just because of how they treated me. They got me 24/7 and they got the best of me. I loved them like crazy. I would do anything for them.

Giving back to them—loving them, being nice in return—led me to one of my favorite projects that I did while I was there. How? Those who I loved working with and showed it in turn wanted to work more with me. Our mutual respect and caring lifted us all up.

To clarify, operating from a place of love and kindness does *not* mean that you need to become a doormat. It does not mean that you don't have boundaries. You must have boundaries, and you must communicate them when needed. Yet, if you operate from a place of love and kindness, you'll find that you won't need to do this too often because when you lead with love and kindness, you lead from a place of strength. And, when matched with inner integrity, you innately *project* strength.

We often think of love and kindness as "soft" qualities. We are so wrong when we think that way. Love is one of the strongest qualities that there is.[5] Just look at history: Mahatma Gandhi led India with love and nonviolence to freedom. Dr. Martin Luther King, Jr. was a leader in the American civil rights movement; not only did he advance civil rights, but he also stands as one of the greatest nonviolent leaders in the world. Nelson Mandela's nonviolent, compassionate acts led to the overthrow of apartheid in South Africa.

These were some of the most powerful individuals in our collective human history, standing toe-to-toe to forces greater than any of us will ever encounter in the workplace. Their awesome power effected changes, but *not* because they kicked ass and took no prisoners; they were powerful because they stood in love and the world bent to their will. That is true power.

Your Intuition Speaks to You through Your Body

❦

The only real valuable thing is intuition.

— Albert Einstein —

INTUITION. IT'S SUCH A BIG, IMPORTANT, AND YET ELUSIVE CONCEPT. But at this point in my life, I find it fascinatingly straightforward.

INTELLECT IS NOT ENOUGH

Oh, to be sure, society places a premium on intellect. Intellect determines your grades in school, which determines which colleges you get into, and in turn college grades may determine the opportunities that you have. Once you land that first job, you quickly see that those in charge are praised for their analytical skills, their intellect, and their logic. You might believe that promotions happen because of it. You may feel you must move into "thinking" mode and stay "in your head." Marion Woodman, a Jungian psychologist, believed that staying in the frenetic energy of the brain can deny your soul.[6] To her, "[s]oul making goes on in the body."[7]

Too often, people think that to be intellectual means ignoring and pushing away emotions. They're led to believe that to be businesslike means remaining calm, cool, and collected in all of your dealings. No outbursts of anger or tears. You may have learned this from a young age. Perhaps your family gave you messages to "toughen up." Or you were taught in school or on the playing field that only sissies cry. The point is that we receive plenty of ongoing reinforcement that displaying emotions is a weakness. Successful, in-control people don't do it.

I'm not saying that we should let our emotions explode in the workplace. I *am* saying that we *can't* suppress them. We have to allow them to happen and, in the process of maturing, investigate to see what they are communicating to us. If we don't understand what our emotions mean—or what to do with them—we *will* suppress them and lead with our intellect.

There are many well-written books on what happens when we suppress our emotions, so I won't tackle that topic here. Suffice it to say that suppressing emotions is often the cause of (or a major contributor to) eating disorders, substance abuse, and alcoholism—or anything that can numb what we are feeling. When we're cut off from our emotions, we also lose our life force. We dull our vibrancy and our creativity. We become robotic. Moreover, disregarding our authentic emotions are, as described by Woodman, a "profound self-betrayal."[8]

Early in my career, I was an attorney at a law firm. Being an attorney required me to rely upon logic, reason, and being in control. I felt that I must operate without emotions to be brilliant and successful. So did those around me. When I went to my five-year law school reunion, the ways in which my former student colleagues had changed were visible and shocking. Some people from my graduating class had shut down emotionally, and it showed. They had aged dramatically, looked pale, and acted lifeless. Yet conversely, others were vibrant (in color and energy) and acted engaged and alive. What made the difference? I discovered that those who remained vibrant embraced all of themselves and channeled their emotions (including passions) into their work.

Yes, intellect is important. But it is secondary to creativity and life force. Creativity and life force are engaged and expressed through emotions. Recognizing, understanding, and channeling emotions helps direct this life force to our advantage.

THE BODY AND INTUITION

This leads me to intuition. What the heck is it anyway? How do you strengthen it (or can you)? You may ask, do I even have it?

Intuition is a huge differentiator in success. This becomes obvious when one studies the business "greats" and dissects what they did differently that let them achieve what they did. Steve Jobs, Jeff Bezos, Marc Benioff —how did they know what they knew? How did they see a market or a product where none existed before? People say they had "great instincts," "insight," "ability to read the market," or "creativity"—all just ways of saying they had stellar intuition.

You have it too. You have probably experienced intuition in some way. For instance, perhaps you were thinking about that ex-boyfriend and all of a sudden you see him dining at the same restaurant as you. Or, as you're driving home, your mother is on your mind and suddenly she calls you. These are little examples of intuition at work. It's just letting you know it's there—even if you aren't paying attention to it.

Throughout your career and life, one of your goals should be to strengthen this inner voice. It tells you what is really meaningful to you. It gives you access to your real values, not just what society or intellect says is right. This inner voice is the voice of your intuition. And it's not just a voice in your mind—it's linked to and speaks through your body.

Too many of us are heads that are disconnected from our bodies. We are humans who have repressed or ignored our feelings. And our feelings originate in our bodies. We prioritize our information systems incorrectly. We value information that comes from the brain; we discard information from feelings or bodily sensations.

Let me give you a statistic that supports reversing this order. Your brain consciously processes roughly forty bits of information a second. This is what you're relying on to guide you through your day. Your body, on the other hand, is receiving eleven million bits of information in a second. *Eleven million.*[9] That is not a typo.

··

**The body knows a link to the world
that the consciousness cannot sense.**

— Tor Nørretranders —

··

Our bodies are the dominant source of true information gathering. What happens with this information that the body gathers? All of it is directed to and processed by the brain. You have no conscious awareness, however, of the majority of this information. By the time it reaches your conscious awareness, this raw data has been reduced or discarded so that you're aware of only a very small fraction of what your body has taken in. Moreover, scientists have established that the conscious brain experiences a half-second delay from whatever it is you have taken in or experienced.[10] This means that consciously, your brain not only perceives far less information than you receive, but it also lags behind what has happened.

To put it another way, your brain still processes all of this information, but you just aren't conscious of it. According to Tor Nørretranders, "The body knows a link to the world that the consciousness cannot sense."[11] We get a "read" on a situation and just "know" what is going on. How do we "read" that hit? Through our bodies and our emotions.[12]

When we shut down awareness of our feelings and sensations, we've cut off the ability to get these intuitive hits. We aren't listening anymore. That leaves only one route to get information—through our brains. On top of that, it analyzes, categorizes, and filters those bits, looking for what conforms to our preexisting ideas and ignoring anything that doesn't fit.

The body is the mainframe that processes the vast amount of intelligence coming at us every moment of the day. The information is there for us to draw upon at any point—provided that we're willing to listen to it. To be willing means that we have to be sufficiently aware of our feelings, emotions and bodily sensations to keep that communication channel open.

Here is an example. In my first year living in Manhattan, I was a wide-eyed Midwestern girl who was learning her way around. My main mode of transportation was the subway, and one day I was riding home on an express train. Express trains don't make regular stops, so you ride for longer distances without the doors opening. On this day, I was wearing my backpack on my back, the car was packed with people, and a homeless man was pushed up against me several times. Suddenly, my body bristled. The hair stood up on the back of my neck and I felt a deep weight in the pit in my stomach. Despite not feeling any tugs on my backpack, I got an intuitive flash that this person was trying to steal my wallet.

What had just happened? Well, my brain kicked in and intellectualized it. It told me, *I didn't feel any tug on my backpack. It's unkind to have that thought about a homeless person—it's stereotyping. Don't move your backpack to the front of you or you'll be silently accusing him, even embarrassing him.*

Still, my anxiety soared and the intuitive hits intensified. Finally, I disregarded the last instruction from my brain and moved my backpack to the front of me. Sure enough, its flap was open and my wallet was gone. While things worked out okay in the end (I got my wallet back), this was a very clear example that I needed to pay attention to urgent signals that didn't necessarily align with the rational information that my analytical brain was gathering and trusting. It also taught me that the brain often interprets those signals wrongly and may even override them.

In his book *Power vs. Force*, Dr. David Hawkins shows that the body not only loves truth and is strengthened by it, but it also gives insight into the kind of information it can access. After more than twenty years of extensive testing, he was able to prove a link between the body and how it responds to information, even if it's information that is new to us. As I mentioned before, his kinesthetic research tested the ability of the body to determine the truth or falsehood of a statement or possible fact. Muscles weaken in response to something false (which includes an untruth or a lie) and strengthen with something true.

Hawkins found that he could even ask a yes-no question about a nuclear physics topic of a thousand people from different countries, backgrounds, education, and economic situations, and the majority answered the question correctly—even people who have no understanding of physics! They didn't have to intellectually know; their bodies did. Indeed, Hawkins asked questions that no one intellectually "knew" the answer to and yet the testers' bodies responded correctly again and again.

How does the body gather the information it responds to? As we know, it's processing 11 million bits a second. It gets this data through our senses,[13] but, as explained earlier, it is also energetically accessing vast amounts of information well beyond what we intellectually (or consciously) "know."

The implication is astonishing. If you shut down your emotions and ignore your body's messages, you have seriously handicapped yourself. You've walled yourself off from the greatest sources of information available to you in any form.

Let's look more closely at emotions for a moment. Perhaps you are one of the many who, by college and thereafter, has not learned to pay a lot of attention to your emotions. You may know when you're sad, angry, depressed, or happy, but you rarely take the time to really check in with an emotion and notice where it sits in your body, or perhaps know the texture of angry that makes it different from sadness, or, most of all, what that emotion may be trying to tell you. Decoding this information is essential. We all must get to know how our bodies speak to us—even if that idea scares you right now.

You may feel resistance to the idea of doing this. Without a doubt, emotions can definitely be difficult. They can feel untamable, messy, or too much—especially if they have been held back for a long time. Yet, once you become open to them and are willing to listen, they will move into a more fluid, understandable state.

Moreover, if you don't resist them, emotions can flow through you in a wave that lasts for only a minute or two, regardless of their strength. It's the resistance from your mind that makes them linger, build in intensity, even fester. Instead, allow the wave to move through you and pass. Then, in stillness, you can ask, *What is really going on here?*

That means shifting into the role of a curious investigator. Just notice. Stay detached. Don't tell yourself what the feeling means or what the story behind it is. Instead, ask these questions to yourself:

> What is it that I'm feeling?
> What are the sensations in my body?
> Where are they occurring in my body?
> How intense does it feel?
> What emotion do I think this is?
> When does this generally show up?

When I'm in possible physical danger (for instance, of getting mugged in the subway), I feel a chilling weight deep in my gut like a heavy rock. It's hard to breathe, and I almost feel like I've been punched. I could label it *scared, danger, warning.* The basic message it's telling me is to beware and *get out now.*

If someone hurts my feelings or I experience a disappointment, I feel a smaller lump in my stomach and my chest feels slightly squeezed. Because this stomach sensation is lighter and accompanied by only a slight constriction in my chest, I know that it's not a fight-or-flight message. Instead, I've learned that it's a message that I feel hurt by something that isn't physically endangering me. Knowing that, I can look at what might have caused it, take steps to deal with that, and get on with whatever else I may need to do to take care of myself.

These nuances are empowering when you're trying to understand what's happening at work. What's actually going on with your boss, your colleague, or your team? What's really happening with that client? The marketplace? The viability of your product line? Interpreting your emotions and the information they're giving you is no longer woo-woo—it's real-world and useful.

You also need this information well before your brain can intellectualize it. And you need to figure out how *your* body sends messages to you, because it may be different from how my body sends messages to me (or someone else's body sends messages to them).

Once you can understand what your body is trying to tell you, then you'll know how to put your brain to work. (You do need your brain after all!) But you just need to make sure that you're working with *all* the information available. Is your gut feeling telling you that something isn't right with your client and that's why the sale hasn't gone through? That's good information. Now, without discarding your intuition, put your mind to work to create a plan to gain the client's trust by understanding why your current strategy isn't working and what would be better; then you can be more favorably positioned to close the deal.

....

*What is done by what is called myself is, I feel,
done by something greater than myself in me.*

— James Clerk Maxwell —

....

One beautiful bonus to this approach is that, because you're keeping your emotions in the mix—trusting them and listening to them—you in turn become authentic, honest, and trustworthy to your client on an instinctual level, just as you would with the horse herd. And you have just significantly upped your chances of success with this client.

To summarize, your body is the largest collector of information you have, accessing and processing vast amounts of it without your even being aware of it. And it communicates this information in emotions, feelings, and sensations. This forms the basis of our intuition about what's going in the world around us. Your goal is to better understand how your body communicates so that you can more readily access, perceive, and process the quality and amount of information that you receive. Your ideal method is to lead with your intuition and then follow up with your brain. This is your winning hand.

Life Truth 2:
You Are Here to Leave a Legacy

❧

Everyone has been made for some particular work,
and the desire for that work has been put in every heart.

— Rumi, Sufi poet and mystic —

THE SECOND LIFE TRUTH IS that we are all here to leave a legacy. Every one of us. Legacy building is written into our *daimon*, our soul's purpose, as James Hillman shares in his best-selling book *The Soul's Code*. Hillman postulates that from birth, we each have within us an "acorn" that holds all that's needed for us to become our version of an oak tree. It's individual and specific for each person. Included within that acorn is the knowledge of what set of experiences we need to have in order to unlock, form, and realize our unique contribution to the world and the perfect expression of our gift. Realizing one's fullest self does not require that we come from a great family life, have all the best chances in the world, or attend the best schools. Instead, each of us is hardwired (through our acorn) to seek out the set of experiences that will give us what we need along the way to reach our potential.

My work with thousands of professionals, many of whom are reaching the top of their careers, validates this theory. Within the life trajectory of each person is a set of experiences that shaped them. Those experiences prepared them to deliver whatever it was that only they were capable of doing.

The same is true for you. I believe that your gift—whatever it is—is something that only *you* can deliver. Every experience that you've had in your life (and will have) has contributed and will help shape and prepare you for what you are here to give. If you leave this world without delivering on your legacy, the potential of it goes with you. Your mission, therefore, in this lifetime is to deliver what you came here to do. It is the mission that you signed up for when you came into this life, and it is the reason you're here.

Legacies come in all shapes and sizes. There are those of Albert Einstein and Alexander Fleming (the discoverer of penicillin), who made scientific or medical breakthroughs. Some have built corporations that employ thousands, such as Jack Welch of General Electric. Others have changed the way people live, such as Steve Jobs, founder of Apple, and Marc Benioff, founder of Salesforce.com. These are well-known business-related legacies. But legacies can take many other forms.

Consider Jane Goodall and her work with gorillas, where she raised awareness about these majestic animals and helped create conservation sanctuaries for them. Consider Geoffrey Canada, the creator of the Harlem Children's Zone: His mission is to break generational poverty cycles with unique educational programs that prepare and empower children from poor neighborhoods to complete college. Consider Maya Angelou, an award-winning author and poet; among her many firsts is *I Know Why the Caged Bird Sings*, the first nonfiction best seller by an African-American woman.

Your legacy could lie in how you parent or create a partnership. It could be writing a memoir that keeps a bit of history alive or composing a song. It could be your ability to reorganize your company's department in a way that improves the lives of employees. It could be a single act of kindness that made another person believe in themselves and live again. There are so many possible variations.

How do you know what your legacy will be? Another way to put this question is to ask yourself, "What is my purpose?"

My experience and belief is that there is something inside of you that already knows (the acorn), and that you find out what it knows step by step. In fact, I believe that by about the time you are fifty years old, you will have gathered enough information to reflect on, look forward, and determine what you are here to deliver.

....

Your job on this journey is to gain an understanding of what you want your own legacy to be.

....

I'll illustrate this with my own life. I grew up in an inner-city area where many of my friends came from disadvantaged circumstances. Few people in my school went to college. My parents are loving, hardworking Midwesterners who adored me immensely and taught me to trust myself. They had a strong belief in God (or spirit). Although my father didn't finish high school and neither parent went to college, they both value education (my father loved to play logic games with me). They both are compassionate, caring people who always believed in me and supported my ideas. They often said that they knew I'd make good choices, whatever they were.

I did indeed go to college, and after that I went to law school and became a lawyer. But after all that education and training, then I discovered that I hated practicing law. Fortunately, I had enough trust in myself (thanks to my parents and my faith) to quit law when I realized it wasn't what I was *supposed* to do. That's when I moved to New York City because my inner guidance told me that I should be there. But at that time, I didn't even know what kinds of jobs were available. I became a headhunter because I figured that, if nothing else, I could learn what jobs I might like. In fact, I became curious about and then obsessed with what kind of jobs are out there, where those jobs exist in organizations, and what kind of skills you need to get them. Eventually, I became a consultant who helped companies restructure their recruiting departments and determine how to select and retain high-performing employees.

I left consulting when I was hired into a job created specifically for me. I oversaw all recruiting, learning, and development, as well as succession planning and many of the internal diversity activities for a Fortune 500 company. Some of these areas required building and rolling out programs that hadn't existed before.

This role was basically a culmination of everything I had learned up to that point, both personally and professionally. It took advantage of my childhood immersed in a multicultural community, which gave me a thorough and personal understanding of what it means to be socially and economically disadvantaged. I intimately understood what types of jobs existed in organizations and the typical skills required to do them. My research experience gained when I was a lawyer ensured that I could find the best candidates for particular positions. I could also determine what types of jobs across the company required similar skills and thus build robust, creative, and innovative succession plans. I understood what competencies were needed at each level, where gaps might exist when someone was promoted or left to take another job, and how to identify learning needs.

Additionally, I was adept at looking at a large, complex organization, understanding multiple strategies and challenges, and prioritizing learning plans and resources. I knew how to do all of this on a large scale, work effectively with senior executives, and roll out programs successfully, all because of each life step I had taken up to this point.

Looking back, there's no way I could have ever created a life plan that got me to that job. In fact, the job didn't even exist before I joined the company. And I could never have known at an early age what I would even be good at or love to do. But, by trusting myself and making a move one step at a time, my path unfolded before me.

It also led to my insights about the three different stages of a career. In the early years, I gathered information. I learned about myself—including how to trust myself. Mid-career, I had a great sense of what I was good at doing, what I liked to do, and what I wanted more of. That gave me the ability to imagine and articulate what fit me. So, by the time I interviewed with this last company, I was clear on what my skills were and what I was most interested in doing next. Thus, I got to help create my position. Now, at fifty-plus years of age, I have a clear perspective on my legacy, which builds on everything I've done and learned.

Your job on this journey is to gain an understanding of what you want your own legacy to be. Just as with Life Truth 1, there are five principles that will contribute to the development of your legacy.

A Career
Is an Evolution

⟨✦⟩

*The people who get on in this world are the people
who get up and look for the circumstances they want,
and, if they can't find them, make them.*

— George Bernard Shaw —

I HAVE HEARD "CAREER" DESCRIBED as many different types
of things—a ladder, a lattice, a matrix, and so on. And in all of
these metaphors, it is something you climb. This implies that
you're always trying to move uphill and that often the climb is
tough.

In contrast, I believe that a career is an evolution. You start
at one place and your career evolves over time in a natural pro-
gression. I agree with the metaphors that your career may evolve
in many directions. But you won't always be climbing up. You
could be stepping over diagonally or laterally or in some other
motion. You will change and your ideas about what you want to
do next will also change. Moreover, as you change, so does the
world. We're all evolving—as we should—together. Therefore,
the possibilities of where you or I may end up are endless. And
sometimes, the world moves to meet you where you are.

"Career as an evolution" is a relatively new concept.
When my parents were young, it was normal to start with one
company in an entry-level position and stay with that company
for all of one's career, hopefully rising in the ranks over time.
For example, you might start in sales and retire as a sales
manager. Or you might start out in the accounting department

and, with luck, eventually become its chief financial officer. There were set roles, steady slow movement, and a linear culmination to a career. Jobs (and careers) had little potential for growth into new types of jobs. The human expression of talents and creativity had to fit within those functional categories; those that didn't manifested in other activities such as volunteer work or hobbies.

Today our options are vast and ever-changing as never before. We are also living longer. Our priorities and values change over the course of our lives. For the first time, the opportunities for expression in our work can evolve with us as we choose to stay in the workforce longer.

If you're just starting out, you should not be looking at your first, second, or even third position as assurance that you're on the "right track." Your responsibility is to focus on what you're going to learn in the role. Learn everything that you can, do a great job, and keep an eye out for when it's time to look at your next position. This doesn't necessarily mean that you should job-hop, however. You'll probably find that you can get a few good years out of that first gig and parlay that experience into a promotion or a different role at the same company (meaning that it will naturally evolve into the next phase of your career).

When you left college, you may have felt both driven and hopeful. You were moving out of an environment that you'd mastered, so you believed you were in mastery. But your mastery was theoretical and not yet proven in the real world. So, when you got your first job, you found yourself being treated as a beginner. That wasn't a bad thing. Being a beginner lets you make mistakes, ask for help, and experiment. People just starting out in the workforce need to use this time to do just that.

When I first moved to New York City, I had a very good friend named Kelly, who had recently moved there as well. She had worked in retail in her hometown for her first year after college and now had started in a retail position in Manhattan. She wanted to transition to a corporate job in the fashion industry, but her postcollege work experience totaled only two years. Over the course of the next year, she'd lurch from one interview to the next. The interviews themselves seemed to go well, but she'd never get a call back.

It turned out that Kelly had decided that she was ready for (and so *only* wanted) a managerial position. In her interviews, she made it very clear that she felt her skills were appropriate for that level of position—and that other positions were beneath her. This attitude killed her interviews. She had overestimated both her skills and what a reasonable entry-level job would look like for her at a company. Moreover, she focused only on the title and not on the range of experiences that she'd like to have.

After a year of trying, she lowered her expectations and eventually landed a temporary, entry-level public relations position with an independent agency where she strived to do her best. Within a year, this role led to a public relations position at a major fashion house where she did get the chance, in time, to rise to a manager-level role. The moral of the story? Take the entry-level job, do your best, and have patience. Your career will evolve.

If you're in mid-career, you likely have experienced a number of changes in yourself, and your jobs have probably morphed quite a bit. You may have gone from one industry to another, or from one functional area, like human resources, marketing, sales, or finance, to another. You may have even—like I did—jumped ship entirely from one career area to something totally different, as well as to something that had nothing to do with your degree.

All of this is good, as long as you make these changes *naturally* and you learn more about yourself and what is right for you. We'll talk about this more later, but for now, I want to plant the seed that your next move should be based on a combination of what you *want* to learn next and—most important—what *feels good*. You should always be moving toward things that feel good to you and that, as we discussed earlier, align with your internal values and goals.

The biggest win often comes in midlife. There is something magical and wise about this stage of life. You get to look at all the evolution that has happened, add up the skills that you've acquired, and begin to craft the next half of your life. What you create from then on will be beautifully suited to you and will let you deliver on the promise that came with you at birth. Just know that it's an evolution to get there: gentle, flowing, purposeful, and ever-changing.

It's Never
about the Money

Stop chasing the money and start chasing the passion.

— Tony Hsieh —

ANOTHER PRINCIPLE OF THIS LIFE TRUTH is that it's never about the money. Ever. This is not to say that money isn't wonderful to have—it is. But it's not what most people want when you really get down to it.

Just so that there's no confusion, I want to get out on the table that I LOVE money. Love it. I love to earn it. I love to save it. I love the freedom that it allows. I'm a big fan and want *you* to have all you desire too. In fact, I believe you deserve it. My hunch, though, is that you might want something *more* than just money.

When you leave college, you were probably eager to strike out on your own. You wanted be self-sufficient; you were looking to thrive and be able to afford things you'd only dreamed about. Naturally, you may have focused on your earnings and how a job fiscally supports you.

As we progress in our careers, our responsibilities increase. Our tastes get more expensive. And we find that we've increased our earning capability along the way. We may now be hoping to establish a home, college funds, family vacations, or a nicer lifestyle. Our tastes don't stay static and they do tend to increase (usually not the other way around). All of which, of course, requires money and that we continue making more and more.

Subtly (or not so subtly), we've absorbed a tremendous number of ideas and opinions about money from our families, society, and the media. We attach a lot of meaning to money: security, safety, success, worthiness. It can't help but be a loaded topic. So, it's no wonder that a lot of focus is placed on money in professional life.

Yet, in spite of all these pressures and focus on money, what I have found again and again is that it is never *really* about the money. Oh sure, we all need enough for the basics. We need a decent roof over our head, food on the table, and clothes and such. In other words, no one is willing to put their family at risk by working for free. But if you're reading this book, I'd wager that you have the basics covered and you're looking for truths that will support you in improving your life. Let's just assume that—in this moment as you read this page—that you have what you need for this day.

Here's an example. Jack is married with three kids, one of whom is severely autistic. He and his wife have a great relationship. He is the sole provider. He works in Manhattan and lives in upstate New York, where his autistic daughter attends a private school that supports her needs. He is working on his third start-up business. He's incredibly great at building these businesses, but this type of work demands a lot of his time. Jack gets home late at night and he's exhausted.

So now, he is talking to a corporation who wants to hire him to use these skills within their business. But they're stuck on compensation negotiations. Jack wants more than they will put on the table, the company won't budge, and they're both at a standstill.

I talked at length with Jack about his options and, in particular, the money. Setting aside both this particular opportunity and the money piece, I asked him, "What is it that you really want if you could write your own position?" He replied, "Work that will stretch me and let me build things. The ability to work with talented people. The chance to make an impact. The ability to have—even a little—more time at home. To feel part of an organization where I will stay for the long term."

Notice that he never said anything about **money**.

When I brought him back to the money question, he said that he wanted to be able to provide for his family so they would be comfortable. He did not say he wanted to support a lavish lifestyle. He wanted to make sure he could continue to send his autistic daughter to the private school that was really helping her. As far as the exact amount, he was willing to consider a smaller salary as long as he could do these things and the opportunity gave him most of the things he wanted to do in his career, meaning the things he named when I asked him to write his own position.

This example allows me to make several points. First, what people want most in their job is an *experience*. They want to feel stretched, appreciated, part of an organization, and respected. And they want to feel that they've been responsible in their personal life obligations. These are the basics. If the position will not provide either of these, the role will either be short-lived or the person will be miserable. Who cares how much you make if you're bored and don't feel like you're appreciated or listened to at the office? No one wants that.

Sadly, many companies miss the boat on how to really negotiate. I mean *seriously* miss the boat. This company never asked Jack what mattered to him. In failing to do so, they lost the chance to show how all his intrinsic desires might be met or exceeded. They didn't see that if he could have those things, he would be willing to take a little less than he was asking because the quality of his overall life would improve.

Now, there is one caveat that I need to insert here. I don't want to create the impression that companies can offer a really low compensation based on the intrinsic characteristics of the job (such as the experience) and then keep someone at that low salary. A highly talented professional is worth every cent they make. To keep someone like Jack, the company will need to pay him fairly and competitively over time.

The intrinsic value proposition is strong only when it doesn't tip to the point where the company severely underpays someone. People who aren't compensated fairly for their skills will leave because they feel responsible to do better for their families (and they can). They will also leave if they feel that the company does not value them, could pay them more, and simply aren't. When a company can afford to compensate better, at some point in the relationship money becomes an expression of how a company values individuals and that they matter. We all want to feel like we matter.

....

Find out what really matters to you and negotiate for those things. Remember: It's always more than money.

....

The third point that I want to make—the big one—is that Jack now has some valuable information about what he really wants. He's defined for himself what really matters and where he's willing to be flexible. He can take that information and negotiate a *great* deal for himself. If this company won't meet his terms, perhaps it's not the place he wants to be after all.

As I've said before, it's almost never about the money but usually about the essence of an experience that we want. We want to feel secure, feel that we're good providers for our family, feel appreciated, and feel recognized. There are numerous ways to obtain these feelings. Money is only one of them, and usually it is the one that provides the least. Often, we get stuck on money because in the pursuit of it, we're giving up something that we really want (like time with our family), so we feel that we need to be paid for that important thing that we've given up. Or we get sucked into the cultural conditioning that money demonstrates "success" or the idea that it will buy the things—the external markers—that prove to others we are successful.

The bottom line: Figure out what really matters to you. What really matters usually has a "feeling state" to it, such as wanting to feel like you're a good provider. Negotiate to make sure you get those things first and as many of them as you can. At the same time, know what you're worth. Be clear on what you're willing to trade off so you have a bottom line set of numbers for yourself. Knowing your worth is different from believing you have to make a certain salary to be considered successful. Your sense of your worth should be based first on a deep knowing that you have value in and of yourself, and only then second on data on what others are paid to do similar roles.

When you negotiate a new position this way, the most amazing things happen. You will be happier because you've secured for yourself the things that really matter to you. You will feel more appreciated because you're being paid in more than just money. You are willing to work harder and do more because your desires are truly being met. In turn, you are the person that people want on their team, want to promote, or want to hire. Hence, the money keeps coming on its own.

Because the thing I've noticed about money is that it's like people: It doesn't want to be around needy, grasping people who are insecure and are using it as a prop to make themselves feel better. Like you and me, it wants to be around vibrant, alive individuals. It's drawn to those who appreciate it, enjoy it, and see it for what it is: an exchange of energy.

Mistakes Are
Full of Opportunities

Where you stumble, there lies your treasure.

— Joseph Campbell —

No one wants to make mistakes. I don't, and I bet you don't either. I'm not sure if it is something that is part of our human makeup, but our drive to avoid mistakes starts at a very young age. I think that it may be a conditioned response. When we were young and we made a mistake, it generally meant that we got in trouble. We found ourselves in trouble whether we made the mistake consciously or unconsciously.

Once, when I was in grade school, I went home for lunch and returned with flowers for my teacher, but not before I'd seen another flower that was so beautiful that I wanted add it to the bunch. Unfortunately, it happened to be from someone else's yard—that of a house next to the school, and yep, I picked it. I was young. I wasn't really thinking about anything other than surprising my teacher. I certainly wasn't thinking that it was stealing. In other words, it was an unintentional mistake.

The moment I plucked the flower, a teacher ran from the school parking lot and yelled at me. Not only did the other students witness this, which shamed me horribly, but I was also punished by losing my right to be a crosswalk patrol person, a very coveted role for a grade-schooler. I was made to go back and knock on the owner's house door and apologize. The home-owner said it was okay and that I could keep the flower, but I no longer cared about it. I was already scarred, having been acutely conditioned not to want to get into trouble ever again.

I've seen this in my kids as well. My older son is a rule follower. Since he was little, he was the compliant kid who would obey the rules and wanted to do a good job. However, starting in second grade, he picked up a habit where he lied about almost everything. He couldn't seem to help it. He would easily slip into a lie and defend it to the end. This phase lasted a couple of years and it drove me crazy. I finally got to the root of where this behavior came from; it showed up any time he felt that he might get in trouble. He straight-out told me that he was so afraid of getting in trouble—over anything—that ironically, he'd rather lie and potentially get away with it, even if it meant possibly getting caught in the lie.

While such avoidance behavior is completely understandable, it can sabotage your career. First, being fearful of and avoiding mistakes will never allow you to be a beginner. Being able to be a beginner is crucial at many stages of not only your career but your life as well. When you allow yourself to be a beginner, you ask questions, you research, and you stay open to answers and options. This way, you're not overly attached to one way of doing something. This allows you to not only learn from everyone around you but also to learn very quickly.

Second, once you let yourself off the hook from ever making a mistake, you're suddenly freer to take the risks to make a better product, decision, or outcome. You can innovate. And, if you're truly open and honest with your bosses or companies that you're trying something new and doing your best, you've cleared the way to give the situation your best shot.

Yes, there will be times when your best shot had better be spot-on. If you're creating a report for your board of directors, your statistics had better be checked, double-checked, and triple-checked. No room for error there.

But remember that not every part of a job requires perfection. Most of the time, a job requires that you get things done while creating and hopefully innovating. Innovation requires the ability to make a mistake and learn from it. Live in fear of making a mistake and you'll never create anything new or innovative. At best, your work will be vanilla—nice enough, but hardly exciting.

SEIZE THE OPPORTUNITY TO LEARN

Mistakes always offer the opportunity to learn. Always. When you make a mistake, look for what you can learn. After you've achieved enough emotional distance, find out what part you played in that mistake. There is usually a lesson in it, and if you're willing to learn, that lesson will serve you well.

Pam is highly driven and successful. When she was in college, if she felt overwhelmed, she would become laser-focused on delivering everything in a fast and furious style. She'd get the job done. But afterward, she'd sleep for days. Since she got the job done at the expense of sleep, she never addressed how she coped with being overwhelmed. She also ignored that she often irritated colleagues when she went into hyperactive mode, as well as the fact that she sometimes got sick afterwards.

After she moved into the senior ranks, she would still resort to this way of coping when she felt overwhelmed. At one point, she was given the task of conducting an audit for one of the departments, which once again sent her into overdrive mode. She did what she'd always done: She drove her team into doing all-nighters, bulldozed others for information that she required, and demanded immediate support to get everything to completion. As a result, everyone who touched her project had their work life significantly disrupted.

The audit was completed on time, but the company didn't deem it a success. Instead, her boss sat her down and reprimanded her. Her behavior to her team and those she interacted with was viewed as aggressive and unproductive. She was warned that she needed to change her management style to one that exemplified better leadership, planning, and teamwork.

In other words, she had made a mistake.

Pam realized that here was an opportunity to review what happened and figure out her role in it. She could have said the deadlines were too tight. She could have said that her boss overreacted. She could have said that it was the employees' fault for not working more efficiently. Instead, she saw the pattern that *she* had created for dealing with overwhelming tasks. She let herself see how it didn't work in this environment, how it was viewed by others, and how it affected her physically (and by now she was experiencing stress-related health problems). Looking at her role and how to correct it became her opportunity to raise the bar on her management style.

When you are confronted with having made a mistake, ask yourself how *you* contributed to being in this position. What did you know that you ignored? What should you have done differently? What can you do differently next time? I believe that we're all naturally programmed to want to do a good job. You are trying your best. So, when a mistake happens, be upfront with yourself. Are you ready to make the changes that need to be made? Are you willing to review your part in what happened? If you can, you'll be able to up your game quickly.

When you get lessons like this, it's important for you to resolve them right away because if you don't, they'll continue to show up. What needs to be changed will come up again and again, and each time it will mirror for you what isn't working. The longer you ignore what you need to look at, the louder the backlash and the bigger the lessons become—as with Pam who finally suffered health problems and was reprimanded by her boss.

DON'T BLAME OTHERS

Lastly and most significantly, mistakes are often the platform that lets us show up brilliantly. Let's say that you're on a team and you make a mistake. Most people would not want to take the blame; they'd want to point the finger at others to deflect it. But the person who is willing to say "Hey, that was me, that mistake is mine, and I'll make sure it doesn't happen again" is the one I want on my team. I can trust this person. They have proven that they're responsible and truthful.

Sometimes things fall apart and it *is* someone else's mistake. You may know what I'm talking about—maybe the boss got in a tight spot, or a colleague is stuck, or the company is facing a crisis. Being willing to step in and offer help instead of playing the blame game shows that you're a team player who wants to help solve the problem, not add to it. It demonstrates that you're reliable in a crisis and can be counted on to help. And you're proving that you are a person anyone would want on their team.

LEAVING IS JUST AS IMPORTANT AS A PROMOTION

⊱❧⊰

If you're brave enough to say goodbye,
life will reward you with another hello.

— Paulo Coehlo —

WHEN WE THINK OF PROGRESSING IN OUR CAREER, we generally think of being promoted. Often our hope is that we have found the company where we will spend the rest of our lives growing, being recognized, and being rewarded well. But the fact is that people change jobs many times, especially during the early and middle years of their careers. The Bureau of Labor Statistics released a study in 2012 showing that the average person born in the latter years of the baby boom would have worked eleven jobs between the ages of eighteen and forty-six.

In addition to changing jobs to advance a particular career, your personality and needs will change. The changes in you won't always match the culture of the company you've joined. And there may come a point when you realize that it's time to pack up and go. One of the biggest skills most people need (and lack) is knowing when and how to leave—because leaving can be just as important as a promotion.

WHEN TO LEAVE

There are obvious reasons why people choose to leave a company. The easiest, most pleasant one to think about is getting an offer from another company that you can't refuse. In that situation, while having the "I'm leaving" conversation isn't comfortable, it's fairly easy to do and you have a bright, shiny new opportunity waiting for you. This isn't so complicated.

It does get complicated when you *need* to leave. There are a few situations where this is the case. You may need to leave because *you* have changed. The company, position, or boss may have been a good fit when you started, but now you've developed as a professional, individual, or spiritual human being and it no longer feels right.

For example, when you started your career, you may have loved the hard-charging, all-night, communal environment of the first company you worked for. You may have thrived on a lack of infrastructure that created spontaneity and freedom. You might have lived for those all-night jam sessions that alternated between playing Xbox, programming, and holding conversations with your colleagues about saving the world. Then you turned thirty (or forty or whatever) and suddenly you have no interest in an all-nighter ever again.

At this phase of your life, you may be married or in a committed relationship. Maybe you have kids. You want to be home at a certain time. You want to be able to get to the office, put your head down, do your work, and not have to socialize in the same way. The company is always what it has been and what you used to love, but you, on the other hand, have changed. It's what I call a "no-fault misalignment."

What else could make you need to leave? Plenty: a toxic environment, low morale at work, or perhaps an abusive boss. Or you may have a kind boss who doesn't know how to support you or how to help you grow. Perhaps you realize one day that you're in a stagnant position with no opportunity to move up or enhance your personal growth. Maybe you realize that you can't bear to go into the office.

The point is that there will be times when you find yourself in a company that's not so great to be a part of, or you have a boss who's not so great to work for. Perhaps things were fine when you joined, but now *they've* changed—your boss, the department, or the company culture. Or maybe you were recently hired but had no idea how the company operated when you joined. Now you've woken up to the fact that you don't want to be where you are.

I call these instances of "misalignment shock." *You* have remained the same in both cases, but either something at the company changed and you've been made alert to the fact that it's not a good fit for you now, or you didn't have all the information you needed when you were hired. This misalignment, in other words, comes as a shock to you. Frankly, this happens more than companies would like to admit. I've found that it seems to happen at least once in every career.

....

The cave you fear to enter holds the treasure you seek.

— Joseph Campbell —

....

What is fascinating to me is how difficult it is for people to let go, even when the fit is so obviously wrong. Perhaps they hope that conditions will change within the company or that their boss will change. Or they feel comfortable in that place where they used to fit so well, even if currently it isn't ideal or even sustainable.

Leaving is hard, and they don't know if they have the courage to do it. This can be especially true for those of us who are over fifty and have concerns about being able to find another position due to our age. And finally, most people need to think they are moving *to* something before they can leave even a bad situation.

Despite the fact that people change careers many times, when professionals leave (or are asked to depart) because of either type of misalignment, almost no one does it well. In fact, most people are terrible at it. But it *is* possible to leave on your own terms and feel good about it. Let's look at two scenarios.

People who stay too long or overstay in a misaligned situation tend to mentally check out eventually. You get bored. It's too easy. You don't want to raise your hand for that special project because by now, you've done one similar to it on three other occasions. So, you just do your job as it is—but even that is slowly killing you. Or it becomes obvious to everyone else that it's not a good fit anymore; it may even look to them like you're not doing your job. For instance, you leave by 7 p.m. because your family life demands you be home, but the office remains in full-force mode and so you look like a slacker. After six years of all-nighters, you stop participating in them. In your opinion, it's a waste of time. In everyone else's opinion, you're slighting them. The net result: You look like the bad guy.

In the case of the no-fault misalignment, the key is to be honest with yourself that it is time for you to move on. This can be hard; it's a bit like leaving the nest or deciding not to hang out as much with your best friends from high school or college. You owe it to yourself to recognize that you have changed and make the adjustments needed to continue to grow.

The easiest way to help yourself get ready to leave is to start talking to other companies in the marketplace so you can see what else is out there. These don't have to be formal interviews; I suggest that they *not* be, at least in the beginning. If you feel loyal to your company, you may have a hard time moving directly to this interview phase. So—ease into it. Just reach out, network with others, and ask if you can buy them coffee and pick their brains. Tell them that you're doing some long-term career planning and that you'd love to get their insights on where you might go from here. You're not actively looking—you're just gathering information. This sets up a no-pressure conversation for you and the other person. You get to research, explore, and build a vision for what can be next. That vision will start to fuel your desire to move to the next step in your career.

With misalignment shock, on the other hand, you need to act quickly. Most people don't. Often, they're devastated when they realize that the job they thought they wanted is a poor fit. But the longer you stay in an environment that does not fit you (especially if it is toxic), the more you lose your spirit and your edge. We tend to want to stay, let the shock wear off, and see if maybe we were wrong or something will change. Don't do that.

You must also be realistic about your situation so you know how to navigate out of it. First, look at what you missed. Do you have a blind spot that kept you from seeing what was in front of you? Was your to-be boss berating a colleague in front of you and you chose to ignore it as maybe something that person deserved or something that wouldn't happen to you? You need to identify these blind spots—all of the ones that show up in retrospect—so you don't repeat them.

But maybe you didn't miss any telltale signs. Everyone you met talked the company up and said how wonderful your boss is. Take a hard look at the interview process and determine what you could have done differently to dig out the information you needed to make a better, more informed decision. Did you need to meet with more employees? Did you need to probe a little more on why the position was open? Or what the turnover for the department had been in the last year? Did you not listen to your intuition that something was amiss? You must take the time to reflect on what happened because it is a learning experience for you and it will inform you of your blind spots, which—trust me—will otherwise trip you up again if you don't know about them.

Once you take this time to reflect, start determining your exit strategy. Do you have a contract? If so, have the conditions for breaking the contract been met? Did you have another offer that was second-best that you want to revisit or pursue? Do you need to line up alternatives? The old adage is not to leave without something else lined up. This is sage advice for two reasons—because there will be no loss of income and because it's true that you are more marketable when you have a job.

> *Many people are so afraid of "the conversation" that they would rather avoid it at all costs. When they can't avoid it any longer, they deal with it by making the other person wrong. No one wins in this situation.*

There will be times, though, where you simply have to go; perhaps the toxicity is too much and the price is too high to stay until you find a better situation. One of my clients, Robert, was hired by a boutique technology consulting firm to grow its business, which was family-owned and second-generation. The current CEO wanted to scale down her involvement and possibly set up someone to eventually buy the business from her. Robert was ideally suited for this role and was hired on as the president.

After six months, the lovefest went sour. Robert found himself being the point person for all the clients. All but three staff members directly reported to him while the CEO avoided responding to all his emails and calls. He did not have time to grow or improve anything. Worse yet, most of his day was spent handling the negative emotions of personnel who the CEO berated when Robert wasn't around. It was a mess. On top of that, the CEO's husband believed that he could yell at Robert and others in his wife's absence.

The situation was intolerable. Robert knew that he had to leave. However, the days and demands were so long that it was impossible for him to interview for another position while he was still at this firm. Robert was the breadwinner for his family and so could not afford a gap in income. He was truly between a rock and a hard place.

Robert and I talked about his alternatives. He knew that the norm was to have a new position lined up before leaving. But he didn't see how he could network and land another one at the pace he had to keep at this company. He also didn't think he could stick it out as long as it would take to secure another position at the level of his current compensation and seniority. He had already lost twenty pounds and his health was being affected.

This was a decision that he needed to make for himself. I couldn't tell or coach him what to do—just as I won't for you. My advice to Robert was to get quiet, look inside, and determine what his inner voice was telling him that he needed to do. We had spent a lot of time working on his inner guidance system, which is always your best source for decision-making.

In the end, he decided that he would take a stand for himself and the employees by giving the CEO two weeks to turn her behavior around. If she didn't, he'd leave immediately. She didn't change. He left—without another position lined up.

I absolutely supported Robert's decision. He had looked at his finances and determined that he had enough to give him three months where he could interview freely. He had a good sense of his network and whom to start reaching out to. The most important thing is that Robert felt confident that this was the right decision. He had looked inside and believed that his inner guidance instructed him to leave. He then evaluated the potential consequences and was willing to accept them should they happen.

That confidence was imperative. It carried him through two months where he didn't find anything. He could go back and remember that "knowing" and the surety of his choice. Plus, he could take that confidence into his interviews and not come across as desperate. He believed that he would be supported and that the right position would show up when he needed it. Sure enough, in the first week of the third month, Robert landed a position with a great company, one that was perfectly suited for him.

HAVING "THE CONVERSATION"

Let's assume that you have reached the conclusion that it is time to go. You have accepted it, have done the things I've recommended, and are now at the stage where you need to have "the conversation." I've witnessed a great many conversations where the relationship between the company and the professional is ending. In general, most people are terrible at it. Let's look at how to do it right.

Many people are so afraid of this conversation that they would rather avoid it at all costs. When they can't avoid it any longer, they deal with it by making the other person wrong. So, they gear up for battle. They look for ammunition. They want to show how bad the person or the company is, all the wrongs that were done against them, how that person or company deserves it that they're leaving them and should have seen it coming. They gear themselves up emotionally to confront their employers, argue with them, and demand that they look at details and admit to past offenses. They get high blood pressure just from the prep work they have to do in order to sever the employment. And this is true whether it is the company that ends the relationship or the employee looking to leave.

I'm stressed just thinking and writing about it.

You don't have to do it this way. If I can help you change your approach on this one thing, this book has been worth it.

You can avoid the scars that can result from mishandling this conversation.

Here is the secret formula: *It doesn't matter* who is on the other end of the conversation—whether you are the giver or receiver of the "it's time to go" news. Either way, the person opposite you in the conversation isn't happy it's happening either. They want you to remember that *they* are human, that they have feelings, and that maybe they tried their best (even if you would vehemently disagree). Most of all, they want you to not make them the bad guy.

So, you're going to treat this person as a human with feelings, and you're going to act as if you believe that they tried their best. This may sound like a tall order. You may want to argue that the other person doesn't deserve it, especially if you're experiencing a misalignment shock scenario. But you're not doing it this way for them (although they may benefit). You're doing things this way for yourself and the better ending it will give you.

In the case of a no-fault misalignment, if you haven't overstayed, have a heart-to-heart talk about what was great about being there, how it was a tough decision, and how this place will always feel like a home. Believe me, they will miss you, but they will get it.

If you have overstayed, you have some cleanup to do. Own what happened. Let them know how much you've appreciated being there, how much you've learned, and how much this company gave you. Then acknowledge that your life has changed. Say that while you loved being at the company, you know that you can't continue to be an active contributor like you were in the past. You might acknowledge that they probably have noticed that you're no longer the person who can do multiple overtime shifts a week or take on extra projects that require extra work every evening or on weekends. If you're honest, straightforward, and respectful, they will understand.

What about the misalignment shock that occurs when the reason to leave is based on values? Well, that too depends. Did you overlook something critical? Were they really clear that they expected you to work on the weekends, even when your wife was in labor? If they were honest about their environment and expectations but somehow you missed it, you need to come clean. And you can do it with compassion and without making them wrong.

For instance, you could say: "I really appreciate the work ethic and commitment that everyone has at the company. I can see the dedication and loyalty and admire it. While I thought I could sustain the weekend work requirements, what I've realized about myself is that, except for extenuating circumstances, my family commitments require that I be home on the weekends. It would be unfair to the company and other employees if I pretended otherwise, and so, I think it would be best for me to find a fit that better suited me and let you find an executive that matches you better." Win-win.

If you genuinely feel like you were duped, you can choose to tell them so. Or you can choose to proceed as though it were something you were made aware of but didn't understand fully. While you may technically have the right to "let 'em have it" for creating chaos in your life, I've rarely seen situations where it's worth it to say so. Take a look at how doing so would serve you. Are you doing it because you need to get it off your chest and want revenge, or are you doing it because you think that you can help them do a better job in later interviews with others?

Consider, too, whether doing this will burn bridges or potentially impact you in ways you can't see—such as future opportunities with people who have a relationship with this person? Are you in an industry or geographic location where there this individual could have unexpected connections to other professionals that you don't know about? Remember, the goal is to keep you intact emotionally and professionally.

If you choose to call it to their attention, I recommend that you make sure you aren't emotional. Don't let yourself speak from a place of anger or revenge. Doing so will only hurt you because you will carry this anger into the meeting and afterwards. Even if they are in the wrong, the cost to *you* isn't worth it. Instead, as in the other conversations I've laid out, constructively and compassionately discuss what you have to share. Don't make it your mission to make someone wrong—just show how it might have gone better.[14]

Before we leave this topic, there is one last scenario that I'd like to touch on: how to handle it when you're on the receiving end of the-relationship-is-over conversation. I'm not going to address when you've been downsized, when you've stolen something, or when you're being asked to leave for cause. Instead, what I'd like to address is when you're asked to leave because you've overstayed.

This is an emotional situation. Generally, when people overstay, they know it. You probably knew that you had outgrown this position a year ago, have been bored out of your skull, avoided putting in any extra effort beyond the bare minimum, and have been passively (perhaps unconsciously) letting people know it. Anyone who's been in the workforce long enough has seen this happen.

Eventually, if you overstay, you *will* be asked to leave. You can count on it. Even though you may want to deny the situation or draw it out, you won't be able to avoid it. By the time your boss needs to speak to you, management has been mulling over for some time what is going on with you. You may have been doing all the basic work required but something is clearly off. Other employees have now noticed and are talking about it. Your boss knows that something needs to give and that, at this point, it's you who needs to go.

Your boss is not enjoying being put in this position. They're feeling conflicted. It's clear that you're no longer a fit but, instead of owning up to it, you've stayed in your role, hampering everyone else. This has left your boss with the burden of determining grounds (or "cause") for doing what everyone knows needs to happen: End the relationship. Your boss has had to muster up all the unpleasant energy and rationale to justify the break. In other words, they've had to gear up and now you're the target.

You could choose to react with surprise, but this is dishonesty. You've known this was coming. If you fight back, it'll just turn into a bloodbath of accusations where no one wins and you still end up without a job. My best advice—which is absolutely in your best interests—is to lay down your sword and be grateful.

Frankly, your boss is doing you a favor. It's time to get your butt in gear. When your boss pulls you into the conference room to talk to you (they never have this conversation in their office, so they can leave if you melt down), sit in gratitude for the experience that you have had, take stock in the opportunity that this person gave you, and let it go gracefully.

....

Muster your strength to end "the conversation" on your own terms. Then, do it with kindness and respect.

....

Let me give you an example. Larry was hired by a large company to create new intracompany programs. He loved to design and implement new programs and enjoyed the challenge. But, during his third year in the role, he got bored. All the building was complete and his job was now one of maintaining and running the programs he'd created. In fact, the company wanted him to focus almost all his time on one of his least favorite programs. The pay was good and the job was comfortable, so Larry stuck it out.

The problem was that Larry was not at his best when he was bored. He wore his boredom like a shirt. He became slower in performing the things he was responsible for, as well as less effective. Yes, there are two sides to this story, and there were contributing factors on the part of the company and his boss that anyone could say were unfair. However, none of it mattered; the deal was that it was time for him to leave. But he didn't.

Larry tried to stick it out until spring. Then he got the call that the boss wanted to meet with him. Larry had enough foresight to know that his boss was eventually going to have "the conversation" with him. He already knew from previous situations that his boss was not able to end relationships well (as most aren't), so he knew he'd be walking into a fight. He could have gone all out and begged his boss to let him stay, but at this point it would not likely work because his boss had already geared up for the conversation and was on the offensive. If his boss gave him a second chance and it didn't work out, then everyone would have to go through the whole process again, and no one wants to do that.

Larry could have chosen a dozen ways to make a stink. He had some valid complaints with the way he had been treated over the last year. His boss chose to fire him during the holidays (a time when bonuses are paid and no companies are hiring). There was also no basis on which to release him for "cause."

But none of that mattered. Larry was going to be fired. Period.

So Larry had a decision to make—how did he want to end it? What experience did he want to try to have? He and I had discussed this before, and he decided that he wanted to end it in a way that made him feel good about himself and the work he'd done there.

This would require Larry to de-escalate the intense emotions and frustration that he'd experienced around his boss.

This meant that he'd have to consciously decide what he would or wouldn't say, how he would feel, and how he would behave while in this meeting. He also had to be prepared to maintain his composure if his boss had an outburst or the situation went emotionally sideways for either of them.

We decided that Larry should sit in the feeling of appreciation and respect for his boss. Larry knew it was time to go, and he could empathize that his boss was having a difficult time handling how to end it. So even though his boss started by berating him for not living up to expectations, Larry just sat there and energetically sent appreciation and thanks. And then he calmly suggested that they talk about a way to unwind the relationship.

Now, this may sound like a wacky thing to do, but within minutes, his boss dropped the attack mode. Instead of having Larry escorted from the building (which was his usual practice), the boss acknowledged Larry's contributions, noted things that Larry did that no one else was capable of doing, and hoped that there were no hard feelings. It ended with the potential for friendship. Basically, Larry decided what kind of experience he wanted to end with, and, because he chose to hold respect and compassion for the other person, it completely and utterly turned the outcome around. In listening to himself and ending it his way, Larry chose to stand in his power.

This is what I challenge you to do. When you find that you're on the receiving end of "the conversation," muster your strength to end it on your own terms. If your terms are to end in a fighting match—well, unfortunately, you'll probably get that. However, if you signal that your terms are to be respected and acknowledged and to end in kindness—and if you're willing to extend that first—you'll find that you get the last say. Larry did.

Don't Let Others Shrink You

⁓❦⁓

If you are always trying to be normal,
you will never know how amazing you can be.

— Maya Angelou —

OUR LIVES ARE FULL OF RULES. This starts at an early age, when you are given rules by your family. They're not all bad. Rules help you modify your behavior so that you aren't hitting your brother anymore or torturing the cat. But what about the family rule about not making noises at the dinner table? How about the old adage that children should be seen and not heard—you know, the one that you were always in trouble for breaking? The rule that has now made you hesitate to speak your mind?

You learn other rules from society, such as "money is hard to come by." You internalize rules from church, school, and work. You may be told (explicitly or implicitly) that your opinion doesn't matter. Or that you must wear a certain dress or pant size. You learn that behaving in a certain way makes you "bad."

I'm not talking about the basic rules that we all know are good for us as a society, such as not killing or stealing. I'm talking about the rules that are someone else's opinion of how *you* should behave, or what you should look like, say, or do. Rules that, when broken, turn into another person's platform for telling you that you're wrong or should be ashamed.

When we're young, especially, we internalize things broadly, earnestly, and deeply. So, when we bump up against a rule and are told that we don't measure up, we remember. We often think of that part of ourselves as wrong. And, if we're really hurt by the encounter, we'll do anything not to experience it again.

RECLAIM THE BRILLIANT "MISFIT"

I think we often lose a part of our brilliance early in life because of rules. We lose the aspect of ourselves that I fondly refer to as the Brilliant Misfit. At some point in childhood, we were our most expressive selves—until someone made us feel wrong about it and told us that part of us doesn't fit in. That's when the Brilliant part of ourselves became the Misfit.

Take a moment to think back to your childhood. Do you recall a time when you got in trouble? Felt ashamed? When it was made clear that you had done something "wrong" according to the rules? Chances are that you did have a time (or two) like that and that you modified your behavior in response.

One of the first times this happened to me was in middle school—specifically seventh grade. Middle school has its own particular challenges, but this experience was a single incident. I was a kid who loved school. I loved to study. I loved my teachers. I wanted to do well in my classes and be liked by the teachers. I wasn't popular or a cheerleader or the prettiest. And all that was okay with me because learning was my thing.

One day, I went home for lunch and decided that I would sneak into my sister's room and "borrow" one of her T-shirts. I can still picture it in my mind: powder-pink, little cap sleeves, and slightly form-fitting. I felt very pretty in it. As a middle-school girl who was starting to notice boys, feeling pretty was a big deal.

So, I snuck the T-shirt, put it on, and wore it back to school. I felt great. I walked taller, was all smiles, and felt vibrant. My first class after lunch was English, where I sat in the first row. I was happily sitting in my seat and feeling great (like I feel when I have a good hair day now) until I noticed that the class had fallen silent. No one was uttering a sound. I looked up at the teacher and saw why. She was glaring at me and making a *tsk, tsk* sound. She finally said, in front of everyone, "You should be ashamed."

I need to clue you in on one other detail about the T-shirt. It was irrelevant to me at the time, and I hadn't really thought about it. In thin, white letters across the front of it was the word "Bitch." As I said, I was a good girl. I didn't curse. I didn't even *think* about cursing. The word on the T-shirt meant nothing to me; I only saw that this piece of clothing was in my favorite shade of pink. But, in the instant when my teacher declared "You should be ashamed," I was.

In a split second, I sank. *Oh my God!* I thought to myself, my face turning hot. *There are rules. Rules that I didn't know about.* With that realization, I was determined never to feel shamed or clueless about the "rules" again.

On that day, that beautiful, free spirit of a girl (my Brilliant Misfit), who was wild and creative enough to risk getting caught by my sister, got tucked away and put in line. I was going to figure out all the rules, follow them, and control how I was treated. (Hmmm … maybe the early seeds were being sown for becoming an attorney?) I would conform. *She* would be subdued. And this worked … for a while.

Many years later, during my career in New York City, I found myself in amazing environments where I needed to be innovative and creative. While immersed in a problem, I'd get flashes of very out-of-the-box solutions. Wild, free, innovative solutions. Solutions that would work. However, until I reclaimed this part of myself—the part that felt like and was labeled a Misfit—I didn't have the courage to voice those innovations, much less put them in place.

But once I was able to reclaim the Brilliant Misfit part of me, it became one of the winning aspects of what I bring to the table. Frankly, most of my successes wouldn't have been possible without her, but to access her skills, I needed to recall and reclaim that part of me.

....

The great epochs of our life are at the points when we gain courage to rebaptize our badness as the best in us.

– Friedrich Nietzsche, *Beyond Good and Evil* –

....

I'm sure you can think of examples for yourself—the parts of you that someone else made *wrong*. A part of you that someone else said *didn't fit in*. Maybe something happened at home, or maybe it was in school or college. Maybe you were told that there were things that you needed to "tone down" once you entered the workforce. You were told that you were too this or that. Like me, you might have found that you were being put in environments (by perhaps a divine energy) that invited you to reconsider tucking this part away. That is an indication, in fact, that your career needs you to be *all* of you, not a smaller version of you.

COMPANY CULTURES AND WORKING RELATIONSHIPS CAN SHRINK US

One of my early mentors told me that he thought that company cultures "round off the edges" of talent. What he meant was that cultures can take what's unique about someone and ask them to be less than what they are. Having spent over thirty years in business, I have to agree.

I'm sure you've been in a situation in a company where you were either told or heard someone else receive this guidance: "Don't break too much glass." Or you're too loud, out-of-the-box, bold, aggressive (in the driving sense, not in the attacking sense), hard-charging… fill-in-the blank. These messages come from peers, bosses, and other colleagues. I've watched this happen and seen both the underlying sources and the impact that such messages can eventually have on that great new employee.

In my experience, these comments come from several places. One is your peers. Let's say you're blazing a trail and happily working overtime; you may be impressing your boss. But at the same time, you may be irritating, annoying, or even threatening your peers who are comfortable working at their own slower pace. The discomfort you create comes from their feeling that they need to match you—and thus, they'll feel compelled to urge you to slow it down. Your boss may not even be aware of this pressure.

This is a cultural issue. Company culture is strong. It supports the level of performance of your peers, and you're pushing up against it. In a culture that strongly supports underperforming (whether consciously or not), you will find yourself without friends if you don't decide to fit in. Whether they know it or not, they are asking you to play small.

Another source of pressure can come from a boss. This is a strange but true phenomenon. It can even occur when you were hired specifically to shake things up! This pressure to dumb-down can come from your boss's own fears, because they may not want to make a mistake. They may not want to step over a boundary or "break too much glass." Perhaps because they believe the fallout will be on them and not you, they may not feel comfortable taking the lead in a change effort. This fear can manifest in a boss coaching you to slow down and fit in. And they may even ask you to table the change that you were brought in to do.

This problem may also show up when you appear to be shining a little more brightly than your boss. Kelly was a vice president brought in to implement an online sales strategy, and her boss had hired her because of her track record of performance. Kelly had two stellar years and was rewarded with accolades and bonuses. In her third year, the CEO announced his top five priorities. Three of them related to Kelly's work, and he publicly acknowledged her efforts in the area.

A true leader and a good boss would take this as a feather in their own cap for making a great hire, fostering that person's skills, and supporting them in delivering such terrific results. In fact, it would take a true leader to help Kelly show up this way—a leader who is confident in their own right and not insecure about their value. Unfortunately, fear is a common trait. In fact, many successful people are waiting to be "found out" or feel they're faking it when they act like they have it together. It's a phenomenon so common that it has been coined the "imposter syndrome." And it exists at every level. Kelly's boss had it.

Soon Kelly found that her responsibilities were being taken "back" by her boss. In fact, two of the areas that were on the top five list were claimed by her boss. As a result, Kelly's role got smaller, and her contributions and ability to shine were diminished. This is another form of being asked to play small.

Such experiences confuse us, and rightly so. We've been asked to be great. So we give it our all and then are made wrong somehow for trying. Or our successes seem to come back later and bite us in the butt. When this happens, it is not about *us*. It is about the environment that we're in, and we need to take stock on whether it's an environment in which we can still thrive.

....

**The key is to understand how firmly embedded
this attitude is in the culture,
what choices you may have within the company,
and if you'd consider making those choices.**

....

If this happens to you, what can you do? Let's look at each instance, starting with the cultural issue. You will know that it's cultural if everyone seems to perform at the same pace or level. If you perform at a higher level, you get pressure (stated or unstated) to conform from more than one person. You feel alone in the level of your drive, the hours you work, and the caliber of your work—plus, you're generally not acknowledged for any of these things.

If you think this is happening, you need to ask yourself the following questions: *Can I affect this culture? Do I even want to? In other words, is the culture changeable? Is it just within this team or department? Or is it everywhere in the company? If it's just within my group, is there an opportunity to move to another department? Would I want to make that move? Can I make the necessary adjustments to fit in and still thrive?*

The key is to understand how firmly embedded this attitude is in the culture, what choices you may have within the company, and if you'd consider making those choices. If you would consider them, ask yourself: *Can I still feel like I'm growing and making a difference? Does this position still support me? Even if it's not what I thought it was going to be, is there still enough worth there for me to try it?* Oftentimes, we can still feel good about a role that was not as big as we thought. But there does come a breaking point when it's not worth it. Know where that line is for you.

What if the situation has been created by your boss? This one comes as a surprise to some because we tend to think of a boss as someone more accomplished than us and who has all the answers. The reality is that bosses are people too. They have their own desires, dreams, and fears. They deserve your loyalty and support if you're accepting a paycheck from them. They deserve for you to support them to the best of your abilities. After all, that is the job you've signed up to do. These things are true … within limits. The limit is reached when your boss is not supporting your own growth.

What distinguishes a boss who's reacting out of fear of company consequences for being too out-of-the-box from a boss who's afraid of your talent? A boss who's afraid of consequences is easy to spot. They hesitate to implement. Such a boss asks you to go back to the drawing board instead. For instance, Seth was asked to create and implement a corporate-wide mentoring program. He reviewed best practices, talked to divisional leaders, and developed a detailed first draft to share with his boss, Ellen, who was the head of human resources. Ellen listened to the proposal and asked Seth to start all over again. She wanted to him to flesh out certain questions that she thought the CEO would have because she believed the CEO needed to review and sign off on every detail of the program before anything could be rolled out.

Seth made the changes and met with Ellen again, but she was still not satisfied. She insisted that he start anew several more times. In their last conversation, she said that she wanted him to anticipate every question the CEO could possibly ask and, until he was able to do that, it wasn't a complete proposal that she could even show to the CEO. She couldn't say what the CEO might anticipate, and she also couldn't direct him further other than tell him that what he had prepared wasn't thorough enough. After almost a year of this back-and-forthing, the initiative died on the vine.

At first, Ellen supported Seth. She asked him to create the proposal, and she reviewed every version and gave him her feedback. But her hesitation to implement and her extreme fear of taking it to her boss when she might not have all the answers in advance simply killed the project. This is an example of a boss who's overly concerned with the consequences.

In my experience, these types of leaders have their hearts in the right place. Like Ellen, they believe that something needs to be accomplished, and they're willing to start the journey. Where they flounder is around the fear of failing. (Don't we all feel this way at some point?) They weigh the risks and try to see their way clear to implementation (or in Ellen's case, review by the CEO). If they can't find a safe way to do it, they simply table the whole project. After all, it's not worth using their political clout when other things are demanding their attention.

What can you do? You can step into this person's shoes, understand their perspective, and try to help them find a way to make it happen. Seth learned that Ellen might hesitate when she didn't feel that every contingency had been identified and planned for. He learned that when she was fearful of stepping out on a limb, she wasn't always sure how extensive the plans had to be.

The next special project Seth worked on for Ellen was to help roll out a company-wide set of "green" goals. This was new for the company, but everyone was committed to it, and therefore it was a high-profile project. It was a ripe situation that could make any senior executive fearful of not getting it right feel at risk. Seth, however, helped Ellen see how to set things up to accommodate initial mistakes. He helped her build a communication plan that openly acknowledged that there might be mistakes in the beginning. The message was that they were committed to reviewing and improving their efforts and that as a result, it was a work in progress. Thus, Seth and Ellen were able to introduce a program that had a built-in feedback mechanism. People were willing to allow mistakes to happen without calling the program itself a mistake, and everyone had confidence that the program would evolve and improve over time.

Such a situation gives you a great opportunity to mentor upward—you can help reduce risks for your boss *and* learn yourself the art of risk reduction in the process. This is a valuable skill at senior levels that will also serve you well in your career. Plus, it's much easier to see how to reduce risk when you're helping someone else instead of when you're in the hot seat yourself.

Still, the boss who is feeling outshone by you can be confusing; you're usually shining because *they* put you in the position to be able to do so. I'm not talking here about the boss who always lets you do the work and takes the credit. Bosses who set things up this way from the beginning know what they're doing and like to keep it that way. If this type of boss still exists and you're working for one, it's definitely time to make a move. The world is way too large to put up with such treatment anymore.

Instead, I'm talking about leaders who had the vision to hire you and then supported you. They prodded you forward and helped you grow. They let you expand your scope of responsibilities and may have even been excited for you. Then, something changed. It comes across as confusing—if they didn't want you to succeed at first, then you wouldn't have got as far as you have, but now they seem to feel threatened.

What are the signs that they feel threatened? Here are some examples: Perhaps you used to be responsible for four initiatives and now you have only two. Your boss has the other two—and they're the ones most visible to the CEO (or your boss's boss). Or perhaps your span of control once covered thirty employees who reported to you, but now several of those people have been shifted back to your boss—along with the kudos for the group's successes. In other words, once you've achieved visible success, or success is on the foreseeable horizon, it is followed by actions that take your successes away from you and give them back to your boss. Or perhaps the responsibility has been shifted from you to a peer or someone else who reports to your boss and is quiet and unthreatening.

You have to be honest with yourself here. If in fact you blew those two initiatives and did a poor job, then you didn't lose these responsibilities because your boss is feeling threatened. You lost them because you weren't doing your job. You must be able to say that there is *not* a performance issue on your end. Pull in a colleague who is a good friend and will be honest with you and ask their opinion. If there are performance issues on your part, acknowledge them and deal with them. Do it for yourself and get back on track.

Here's an example of what I mean: Brent was hired by a consumer goods company to create a marketing plan. He had never worked for a corporation as an employee, only as a consultant. So, he had no idea how corporate cultures worked or how to navigate them. He was used to coming in temporarily for a project, doing it, and then moving on to the next client once the project was completed. Julie, the woman who hired him, left at the end of his first month to go on maternity leave. Jack, who was her peer, filled in while she was gone.

Brent's conversations with Julie had left him feeling that he had everything under control when she left, and so he rarely checked in with Jack. If Jack's suggestions differed from Julie's, Brent went with Julie's ideas. Four months into the project, the company's annual review process began. Jack led Brent's review. It wasn't a good one, and some of Brent's responsibilities were taken from him and put under Jack's direction. Those responsibilities included high-profile rollouts of marketing pieces into stores.

When Brent came to talk to me, he was understandably upset. He had always had glowing reviews. He was an incredibly talented and hardworking. He had a great relationship with Julie and felt that he had executed her directions to the letter. On the one hand, he was right. He could have chosen to say that Jack had issues and just walked away from the company. But as we talked, it became clear to Brent that he himself had participated in earning this poor review. He didn't ask Jack questions or go to him for his feedback. When he did get it, he then disregarded it. In Jack's eyes, he was neither a team player nor was he trustworthy, and Brent finally realized this.

This issue wasn't Jack's. Brent had some things to clean up. He knew that he could leave and in the process, state all the reasons why it was justified in a way that everyone would understand his position. Or he could be honest with himself about where things had broken down and take on the personal challenge to rebuild his reputation and trust with Jack and others within the company. This latter choice would be the one that, while he had to dig deeply, had the potential to empower his self-confidence and faith in himself. He decided to stay and rebuild. He was promoted the next year.

If you find yourself in a similar situation, look honestly at what you need to own in how your responsibilities were downsized and then determine what your cleanup plan needs to be. But what if you *have* looked hard at your role in the situation and there aren't performance issues? In other words, you did your job well and yet have found yourself losing ground instead of gaining it. As I mentioned before, your boss may feel threatened or unsure about how they appear to higher-ups in contrast to your successes. It happens more often than we think.

At first, people in this situation can be unsure of what's going on. It's hard to recognize what is happening because, although it tends to occur within the span of a year, it doesn't happen all at once. One day, you find yourself questioning what's going on. You think that because this person—your boss—once believed in you and hired you to begin with, they must still believe in you … right? Your gratitude and loyalty make you doubt, even though you have an intuitive sense that something isn't right. There may be a logical reason given for the movement of responsibilities, even though you were handling them without a problem. Even your boss may believe this too.

You will know that you're being marginalized if your responsibilities continue to decrease. You will know it if you're no longer being invited to the meetings with senior staff or are no longer given tasks that put you in the spotlight. And you will know it if your access to your boss is less frequent or becomes harder to attain.

Where does this leave you? First, you want to be sure that you're seeing the situation correctly. You've already determined that your performance record is spotless. Next, take some time over a quiet weekend, reflect, lay out the facts, and determine if you are truly being marginalized. If so, and you still want to work for the company, explore your alternatives. Can you transfer to another department or division?

If there aren't other alternatives, it's time to move on. You must, because if you choose to stay, knowing what you know, then you are participating in playing small. Moreover, you are overstaying. At some point, you won't just be marginalized—you'll be asked to leave.

Executives who experience such a situation often feel angry, hurt, or betrayed. They've given their best, been recognized for it, and then were made out to be wrong for those successes. I understand. They may believe that they're justified in expressing this anger, telling the person off, or crying foul. While they may be right, it won't feel good. In fact, as I discuss in the chapter "Leaving Is Just as Important as a Promotion" about leaving, it will feel awful and get them nowhere.

My goal is to keep you intact and in charge of yourself, your experiences, and your career. The moment you realize that you're being made small, start looking for another position. At the same time, cultivate compassion and gratitude for your current boss. I'm completely serious. I'm not saying that what they've done is right; what I am saying is that they're human. They are subject to the same fears and frailties that you are. And

I'm saying that you should move into the place where you can be grateful to them for recognizing what was great in you, giving you a chance, supporting you, and letting you have the successes that you did, because that is the foundation upon which you will build the rest of your life.

Those are gifts that you get to take with you. If you can leave in compassion and gratitude, you will leave strong and on your own terms. You will make a move from a place of strength and be able to recognize the next role that will let you play to all your strengths. That is the path I want you to be on.

CONCLUSION

The privilege of a lifetime is being who you are.

— Joseph Campbell —

We've set the stage. I've given you two of the biggest truths, each with several key supporting principles that I've learned form the basis of success. Not just on-paper success; I mean the deep-rooted, high-satisfaction sense of success that makes all the difference. I mean the confidence of knowing who you are, knowing that you have the power to direct your life, and knowing that no one can take this from you.

You are here for a reason. By birthright, you are meant to have success and it's based on a blueprint of who you are. It's formulated to match your gifts to your happiness. There is no mistake—You Are a Gift.

Don't play small. Be all of you, with compassion and kindness, all of the time.

Parting Words

These truths and their supporting principles will serve you well in both business and in life. Keeping them in mind, I'd like to share with you some insider secrets important to different stages of your career. Whether you are my client, best friend, or one of my sons, these secrets are what I would tell you matters at each stage.

From all of my experience, I know that there are three broad stages to your career-life: The Early Years, Mid-Career, and Fifties and Beyond. These don't just apply to different age ranges. Each one has different priorities and focuses. And these may not align with what you've been taught that you should do and be.

If you think of your career as an expression of yourself, this will make sense. As you grow older, your interests and priorities change. You get to know yourself better. You refine your tastes and become more selective because of it. When you were in college, for instance, everybody your age was a friend. But later in life, your friends might include the neighborhood moms or the couples who go to the same club. Or it may be the women from your book club or the guys who volunteer at the same nonprofit organization. You may enjoy larger gatherings with your family or you may like quiet nights with just a few friends. The point is that you will evolve in life and so will your career. These three stages roughly follow your evolution.

In my next companion book, I cover these three stages of your life and career in more detail, applying the distillations of truth from this book and what is important at each stage and how. I'll give you specific tools and exercises to help you at each of these stages. And, since we are all "achievers" and like to know that we're doing well, I'll give you markers to know if you're making progress in areas that matter.

Most important, I'll be setting you up for your success, putting you in the driver's seat with your very own GPS system. Or, perhaps more accurately, showing you how to operate the GPS that came with you. My hope is that you realize that it's always there inside you, with the perfect set of directions for every moment of your life.

Endnotes

1   Neil H. Kessler, *Ontology and Closeness in Human-Nature Relationships: Beyond Dualisms, Materialism and Posthumanism* (Cham, Switzerland: Springer Nature Switzerland AG, 2019), 252.

2   Tor Nørretranders, *The User Illusion: Cutting Consciousness Down to Size* (New York: Penguin Books, 1999), 161.

3   Nørretranders, 247.

4   In his book *Power vs. Force*, Dr. Hawkins used kinesiology to calibrate the strength of specific attitudes on a scale of 1 to 1,000 (with 1,000 representing the highest strength possible). Anger, when represented as resentment and revenge, calibrated at 150, whereas love, which is expressed as a forgiving, nurturing, and supportive way of working with the world, calibrated at 500. David R. Hawkins, *Power vs. Force: The Hidden Determinants of Human Behavior* (Carlsbad, California: Hay House, 2002), 68–69.

5   Later in his book, Dr. Hawkins explains that Gandhi aligned with and expressed Universal principles (nonviolence, intrinsic dignity of man, the right to freedom, and selflessness) and thus was aligned with Power. He calibrated the power of the Universal Principles supported by Gandhi at 700! He further shares that Nelson Mandela did the same (Hawkins, 152).

6   Marion Woodman, *The Ravaged Bridegroom: Masculinity in Women* (Toronto: Inner City Books, 1990), 30.

7   Woodman, 31.

8   Woodman, 171. Woodman was a Jungian psychologist whose work focused on healing and connecting to spirit and one's potential through bodywork. Much of her work focused on the "feminine," which is meant as an archetype, not a gender. As she shared, "Body awareness had become an important focus in my analytical practice because of my experience with both women and men who, despite their commitment to their dreams and their own growth, are still unable to trust the process. Their souls are dislocated in their bodies so wounded that the ego's willingness in itself is simply not enough" (from *The Pregnant Virgin: A Process of Psychological Transformation* [Toronto: Inner City Books, 1985], 55).

9   Tor Nørretranders, *The User Illusion: Cutting Consciousness Down to Size* (New York: Penguin Books, 1999), 124–126.

10   Nørretranders, 220.

11   Nørretranders, 324.

12   Nørretranders, 124–126.

13   Nørretranders summarizes research to explain the amount of data taken
      in by each of our senses. He shares that "The eye sends at least ten million
      bits to the brain every second. The skin sends a million bits a second,
      the ear one hundred thousand, our smell sensors a further one hundred
      thousand bits a second, our taste buds perhaps a thousand bits a second"
      (Nørretranders, 125).

14   There is one situation that I want to note. I recognize that there may be
      times when you find yourself in a new situation where you feel you've been
      grievously misled in the interview process, or you may face unexpected
      business issues that border on illegality. I haven't seen this happen a lot, but
      I do know several executives who have experienced it. It's devastating. Not
      only would they never have chosen the company, role, or department to
      which they had they been recruited, but they also had to deal with ethical
      decisions as to whether to stay and clean up the situation or leave. This
      type of situation is not what I'm addressing in this book.

ACKNOWLEDGMENTS

I am grateful to so many people who have supported my journey in writing this book. And even more grateful to those who supported me on the journey that led to the experiences I've had that I can share. While this cannot cover everyone who's touched my life in a way that contributed to *Don't Play Small*, here are a few extra-special people I'd like to thank.

Mom + Dad, thank you for your bottomless love and support. I know I learned "I can do it" from you both. Thanks to Melissa Horton for—well—everything. I'm eternally grateful for how you constantly help me connect to my internal guidance and reach for the stars. A big thanks goes to one of my dearest friends, Angela Mosley, who was the best friend a person could ever have. You were an angel on the planet and I am grateful for how you always elevated me and how you always elevated others. And, thank you to my wonderful sons—Salvatore and Marco. Who knew that parenthood could be such an opportunity to ensure none of us played small?

I also want to thank two people who helped me get this book to you. Jodi Bower—thank you for your constant, heartfelt editing. Mi Ae Lipe—thank you for taking my draft and making it happen! I am so grateful for your editing, coaching, design skills, and production advice (and even more!). I couldn't have done it without you.